W9-AHZ-340

Who's Afraid
of the Holy Ghost?

Who's Afraid of the Holy Ghost?

by
Stevan F. Williamson

HARRISON HOUSE
Tulsa, Oklahoma

Unless otherwise indicated, all Scripture quotations are taken from the *King James Version* of the Bible.

Scripture quotations marked (NIV) are taken from the *Holy Bible, New International Version®*. NIV® Copyright © 1973, 1978, 1984 by International Bible Society. Used by permission of Zondervan Publishing House. All rights reserved.

Who's Afraid of the Holy Ghost?
ISBN 0-89274-916-4
Copyright © 1994 by Stevan F. Williamson
Mighty Wind Ministries
P. O. Box 741906
Houston, Texas 77274

Published by Harrison House, Inc.
P. O. Box 35035
Tulsa, Oklahoma 74153

Printed in the United States of America. All rights reserved under International Copyright Law. Contents and/or cover may not be reproduced in whole or in part in any form without the expressed written consent of the Publisher.

Dedication

Just moments before he stepped into glory, I was praying with my wife's grandfather. As I prayed in the Spirit there beside him, he raised his hands and joined me in his own heavenly language.

When we had concluded, he lowered his hands, looked up at me and said, "When'd you get turned on to that stuff?"

He didn't realize that his own testimony had played a major part in my seeking a closer walk with the Lord. So it was a special blessing for me to share it with him before he made that last big move.

Casey Jones was indeed a unique individual and truly a man of God. His life (and even his death) was a testimony to the Lord. He had shown a boldness for witnessing like few I've ever met. He had led many, many people to the Lord and into the baptism of the Holy Spirit. And through his family, he led me.

So this book is dedicated to G. S. "Casey" Jones. Though I knew him only for a short time in this earthly life, one day we'll be together for eternity. When I step inside those pearly gates, I'm sure I'll hear his voice hollering, "Good News!" And I'll respond with his trademark: "Praisealleuia!"

Contents

Acknowledgments

To my wife, Robin, who showed so much love, patience and support during the writing of this book. Her encouragement and belief in me is a testimony to the Lord living in her life.

To my parents, Fonzy and Lauda, for their never-ending support throughout my life, and for introducing me to my Savior, Jesus Christ.

To Pastor Jack R. Pidgeon, who was instrumental in my receiving the baptism of the Holy Spirit.

To those teachers, preachers, friends and family members who taught me about the Lord and His never-ending love.

To God, Jesus and the precious Holy Spirit, for guiding me throughout this endeavor and for giving me the inspiration, wisdom, patience and endurance to complete it.

Preface

Many Christians have an amazing testimony about being delivered from drugs, drinking and a life of debauchery, but I was fortunate enough to be reared by loving Christian parents who introduced me to the Lord at an early age.

We attended one of the major denominational churches where I learned many basic biblical truths that will be with me forever. That foundation was the platform that shaped my whole life. I can truly testify that the reason I did not forsake God in later years was due to the early training I had received. There is so much truth in that well-known proverb:

> **Train up a child in the way he should go: and when he is old, he will not depart from it.**
>
> **Proverbs 22:6**

All that seed planting and support came to fruition when, at the age of twelve, I received my salvation at a Bill Glass revival in Hamilton, Texas. That was the most important decision of my life.

I don't remember ever being taught much about the Holy Spirit as I was growing up. It wasn't that I was taught *against* the Holy Spirit; He just wasn't mentioned much. So, naturally, I was very skeptical when I first heard of this subject. Yet, I always felt like there was something more, something missing...

After I graduated college, I met and fell in love with a beautiful young woman. She was everything I had prayed for, except for one little detail: she was Spirit Filled!

When I first visited her church, it was very different from what I was accustomed to. I was a little uncomfortable, but I couldn't help wondering how such a wonderful, well-adjusted, intelligent girl would have such strange beliefs. Maybe it was her parents! Then, I met her parents and was very impressed with them. They too were gracious, loving, and intelligent. In short, they were an all-American family! They not only went to church, but were very open in their witness for Christ.

I started going to her church on a regular basis and began to meet the ministers and the congregation. More and more, I was convinced that these people were sturdy and levelheaded. They were excited about Jesus! They were not afraid to talk about the Lord and His influence in their lives. What was it that made them so excited?

By this time, we were married, and I had decided that this "baptism in the Holy Spirit" was a real experience. But, more importantly, I resolved that if God had something more for me, I wanted it! So, I began to ask for the baptism in the Holy Spirit.

Almost fifteen years after receiving my salvation, I received the baptism of the Holy Spirit. It was truly a turning point in my walk with the Lord.

I felt a flood of peace, love and joy that I cannot adequately describe. Even as a Christian, it was the most remarkable show of God's power I had ever experienced.

It was like in one instant all the problems and burdens of a lifetime were lifted off of me. I felt a fresh, indescribable strength flow through me. It was like unscrewing the cap from a bottle of soft drink after it had been shaken. All of that pressure was gone as the Spirit inside of me was released.

There were no earthquakes, no lightning, no thunder. I was the same person on the outside, but on the inside I was rejoicing. There was a difference in my spirit, and I felt my whole countenance had changed. An excitement that I had never experienced was racing through my body. I *felt* power. I *felt* love. I *felt* like I was ready to take on the whole world. I still do!

Receiving the baptism of the Holy Spirit was a tremendous confirmation of everything that I already believed. The Holy Spirit is the Spirit of Truth, and as I opened myself to Him, He confirmed to me that God *is* real, the Bible *is* true, Jesus *is* alive, He *is* the Son of God, and He *did* send the Holy Spirit as He promised.

When the Holy Spirit came into my life, He provided solid proof of the Lord. This gave me more faith than ever before regarding the Lord's master plan. I realized the baptism in the Holy Spirit was real, true, exciting, scriptural, and it is God's will for every believer! If it weren't, the Holy Spirit wouldn't be here.

Almost immediately after receiving the baptism, I felt a prompting of the Holy Spirit to seek out all I could learn about the baptism of the Holy Spirit. I still had many questions, but I had a supernatural Partner to teach me the things of God.

From that point forward, I began to gather questions regarding the Holy Spirit. I collected questions from friends, strangers and relatives, and some from my own experiences. I was fascinated that so many people had so many questions.

As I gathered the questions, the Holy Spirit provided the answers. I began to share with others what He had revealed to me. He began to use me to lead my friends and associates to the baptism of the Holy Spirit, and I rejoiced as I saw them lead others. The Holy Spirit is catching!

A year later, the Holy Spirit made it very clear to me that I was to write a book that would be a blessing to many people. As He so eloquently spoke to me: "Your book will be an open door to many who have not received." You are reading the final product of that assignment.

One basic point the Holy Spirit emphasized was that the book needed to be easily understood. During my personal search for the truth about the Holy Spirit, I encountered too many books that were written "over my head" or were too "deep." In my experience, most people don't want heavy theological prose; they simply want to ask questions and get some answers!

I have tried to arrange this book into a simple, easy-to-read, logical study of the Holy Spirit, using solid scriptural support. My purpose is to thoroughly inform the diligent seeker, yet quickly satisfy the skeptic. I will try to dispel some rumors and clear up some unknowns.

I am a living testimony that the Holy Spirit can do wonderful things in a life when that person is willing to submit to Him. He has used me in ways I could never have imagined. Still, He is constantly teaching me more about God and Jesus. He will be *your* Teacher, too. All you have to do is ask.

My prayer is that this book will help you begin an exciting journey into a deeper knowledge of the Holy Spirit and our Savior Jesus Christ. God bless you!

As the words flow from your fingers, they will find their place in the hearts of others.
— A word of wisdom given to me while writing this book

1

Meet the Holy Spirit!

Who's afraid of the Holy Ghost?

Actually, a lot of people are scared of the supernatural!

Why? Because they don't understand it.

People have an inherent fear of the unknown. Unfortunately, this is probably the greatest barrier to understanding and accepting the Holy Spirit.

Have you met the Holy Spirit? If not, may I introduce you? I'm serious.

If you have never been formally introduced to the Holy Spirit, then allow me to be the first.

Think about it. If you desire to truly understand spiritual things, then you must first *meet the Holy Spirit!* That's why I have devoted this entire chapter to getting to know the Holy Spirit.

You may be thinking, *I just want to get to the good stuff — like speaking in tongues!*

Guess what? The Holy Spirit is the Source of *all* these wonderful gifts. Getting to know Him is truly the most important aspect of finding all the things you are seeking.

I understand your enthusiasm, but bear with me through this introductory chapter. You will be greatly blessed by learning the truth about the Holy Spirit and how He can become a part of your life.

• What is the Holy Spirit?

First, your question should not be *"What"* is the Holy Spirit?, but *"Who"* is the Holy Spirit?

The Holy Spirit is a Person, not a thing. The Bible refers to the Holy Spirit as *He*, not *it*. Specifically, the Holy Spirit is the third part of "the Trinity," which consists of God the Father, God the Son and God the Holy Spirit. Look at what the Bible says:

> **Go ye therefore, and teach all nations, baptizing them in the name of *the Father*, and of *the Son*, and of *the Holy Ghost*.**
>
> **Matthew 28:19**

Most of us tend to lump together all the Scriptures about God. But by searching the Scriptures you will find that the Holy Spirit is shown distinctly as a separate and unique Entity. You will also find that you may have missed many very important promises God has for you.

The Holy Spirit is mentioned throughout the Bible, and the Bible shows us that He has been here since the beginning:

> **And the earth was without form, and void; and darkness was upon the face of the deep. And *the Spirit of God moved* upon the face of the waters.**
>
> **Genesis 1:2**

Keep in mind that the Holy Spirit is referred to in different ways throughout the Bible. He is called *the Holy Spirit*, or *the Holy Ghost*, or *the Spirit of God* or simply *the Spirit*.

Many people skim right over references to *the Spirit* or *the Spirit of God* because they are thinking that this is "just God's personality" or "just plain God." It isn't. The Spirit of God is the Holy Spirit!

True, the Holy Spirit exhibits traits that are in line with God's personality, but that's just part of His nature. The Spirit is a separate Entity from God. No, He is not an "additional" God; He is a separate part of our one true God, as Jesus is.

- **I'm confused. Can you explain "the Trinity"?**

You're not alone! Many people are not familiar with the Trinity. Even many Christians are unfamiliar with it. We sing about the Trinity in many songs and hymns, but most denominations never clearly define "the Trinity."

As I have said, the Trinity consists of the Father, the Son and the Holy Spirit. The Trinity is made up of Three distinct Entities, which are always working together as One. This is a little difficult for us to understand in human terms because it is supernatural. But the Bible testifies to it:

> **For there are three that bear record in heaven, the Father, the Word, and the Holy Ghost: and these three are one.**
>
> **1 John 5:7**

In the above Scripture, Jesus is referred to as **the Word**. (See also John 1:1,14; Rev. 19:11-13.) This "Oneness" of the Trinity is shown throughout the Bible. The following Scripture shows Jesus Himself recognizing that He and the Father are One:

> **And now I am no more in the world, but these are in the world, and I come to thee. Holy Father, keep through thine own name those whom thou hast given me, that they may be one, as we are.**
>
> **John 17:11**

So the Bible says that all Three are One, and Jesus says that He and God are One. It follows then that God and the Holy Spirit are One, and Jesus and the Holy Spirit are One. It may be a hard concept to understand, but let me just say that the Trinity consists of God, Jesus and the Holy Spirit, all rolled up into One supernatural Entity. They are all so closely intertwined that They can't be totally separated.

Here is an example that may help you visualize this concept:

A Light Bulb

There are three main ingredients required to produce light: electricity, a bulb and the rays flowing from the bulb.

The electricity is like God in that He is the Source of power. He is the hidden power in everything we see.

The actual bulb with the glass and filaments is like Jesus. He is the One we can see, feel, touch. Like His disciples, we will believe if we can touch.

The light rays are like the Holy Spirit. He is the One Who actually reveals things to us from the darkness. Just as the light shows us where to find the bulb, the Holy Spirit is the One Who leads the way back to Jesus.

Once we find that bulb, we recognize that there is an even-greater power at the source: the electricity (God). Although we see a light bulb as one entity, we can also see each element as separate, each having its own unique traits.

Now don't get the idea that I am saying there is more than one God. There is one God, Jehovah; one Son, Jesus; and one Spirit, the Holy Spirit. But as the Trinity, They function as One.

- **Is the Holy Spirit a "person" or a "thing"?**

The Holy Spirit is a "Person" in the sense that God is a "Person." Let's look at how the Bible describes the Holy Spirit.

God said, **Let us make man in our image....So God created man in *his own image*** (Gen. 1:26,27). Of course, God is a Spirit, not human like us, but He has His own personality.

Throughout Scripture, the Holy Spirit is referred to as *He*. He has a mind. (Rom. 8:27.) He speaks to us. (Acts 8:29.) He can grieve. (Eph. 4:30.) These are the characteristics of a Person, not a thing. A thing is an inanimate object with no life to it; the Holy Spirit is the very Breath of Life! The key is that He is a Person, not a human.

- **Does He have a name?**

Yes, but not an earthly name like you and me. His name is *Holy Spirit*. He is also called *Holy Ghost, Spirit of God, Spirit of Truth, Comforter, Helper, Paraclete* or simply *the Spirit* — just to name a few.

He goes by many names, but there is only one Holy Spirit.

- **What is the relationship between God, Jesus, the Holy Spirit and me?**

Since analogies worked so well for Jesus, I'll try one now. For a moment, think of yourself as a tree. Your relationship with the Trinity would be something like this:

1. God created you as a seed.
2. Jesus planted you in the living soil.
3. The Holy Spirit is the fertilizer.

The Holy Spirit as the fertilizer helps you to grow and causes your roots to be more firmly planted. He provides nourishment from God's Word and brings revelation that springs forth abundant life. The fruit you bear throughout your Christian walk is the fruit of the Holy Spirit. However, the Holy Spirit does not function in your life without Jesus, just as fertilizer does nothing to a seed until it is planted.

- **The Bible says that the Holy Spirit "descended like a dove" upon Jesus. What does this mean?**

Before Jesus began His ministry, John the Baptist was sent by God to tell people of the coming Messiah. God also gave him instructions to baptize people in water (which is how he became known as John the Baptist).

So that John would recognize the Messiah when he saw Him, God gave him a supernatural sign: he would see the Holy Spirit descending upon a certain one. Through that sign, John would clearly know the identity of the Savior. God's message to him is recorded in the Scriptures:

> **And I knew him not: but he that sent me to baptize with water, the same said unto me, Upon whom thou shalt see the Spirit descending, and remaining on him, the same is he which baptizeth with the Holy Ghost.**
> **John 1:33**

While John was baptizing Jesus in water, the Holy Spirit descended "in a bodily shape like a dove." Since the Holy Spirit is by nature invisible to us, He took shape "like a dove" so that John could see Him settling upon Jesus. Lest there be any doubt about "the dove" being the Holy Spirit, the Bible makes it clear:

> **And the Holy Ghost descended in a bodily shape like a dove upon him, and a voice came from heaven, which said, Thou art my beloved Son; in thee I am well pleased.**
>
> **Luke 3:22**

(See also Matt. 3:16; Mark 1:10; John 1:32.)

This Scripture verse shows the specific event in which Jesus received the Holy Spirit. We know this because of the sign that had been promised to John.

You may ask, "Why did we need a sign, since God Himself verbally confirmed that Jesus was His Son?"

I believe God was making a statement about the importance of the Holy Spirit. Although God audibly spoke, saying Jesus was indeed His Son the Savior, He still considered the imparting of the Holy Spirit important enough to be displayed separately.

There is an exciting truth in all of this. The Holy Spirit Jesus received is the same Holy Spirit we receive today! If you will study the Scriptures, you will see that Jesus did not perform miracles, healings or anything supernatural until *after* He had received the Holy Spirit. Those were manifestations of the Holy Spirit. We too have the ability to do those deeds through the power of the Holy Spirit.

- **People talk about spirits all the time. How many "Holy Spirits" are there?**

One, and one only! Just as God said we should have no other gods before Him (Ex. 20:3), there should be only one Spirit that we worship: the Spirit of God. Other spirits exist, but there is only one Holy Spirit.

> **For through him we both have access by one Spirit unto the Father.**
>
> **Ephesians 2:18**

> **There is one body, and one Spirit, even as ye are called in one hope of your calling.**
>
> **Ephesians 4:4**

(See also 1 Cor. 12:11-13.)

• Are all "spirits" the same?

Definitely not! Most "spirits" people talk about these days have nothing to do with the Holy Spirit.

Often, those who are involved in things like fortune-telling, palm reading and tarot-card reading claim to reach into the spirit realm. Some of them may; but, I warn you, those spirits are not from God!

Do not be tricked by any of them into thinking they are communicating with the Holy Spirit.

Anyone practicing these "arts" may say they are harmless, but don't be led astray.

How does God feel about things like this? Let's look at what the Bible says:

> **Let no one be found among you who sacrifices his son or daughter in the fire, who practices divination or sorcery, interprets omens, engages in witchcraft, or casts spells, or who is a medium or spiritist or who consults the dead. Anyone who does these things is detestable to the Lord....**
>
> **Deuteronomy 18:10-12 (NIV)**

• Where did the Holy Spirit come from?

In response, let me say first that He has simply always existed. Just as God has always been, so has the Holy Spirit. Genesis 1:1,2 tells how in the very beginning the Spirit was hovering over the waters of the earth. As a part of the Trinity, He has been around since there was nothing.

The Old Testament is full of the Holy Spirit's works in the lives of God's chosen men, such as Moses, David, Samuel, Elijah and many others. In those days the Spirit of God was given to specific men and women for specific tasks.

Then in the New Testament we see the ministry of the Holy Spirit being revealed. After all, it was the Holy Spirit Who came upon Mary, causing her to conceive the Child Who would be our Savior. (Luke 1:34,35.)

The Holy Spirit has been an integral part of God's plan since the beginning. He is always on the scene whenever God is doing a work.

Secondly, we are living in a new phase of the Holy Spirit. Unlike the old days in which only specific men and women received the Holy Spirit, today He is available to all believers. On the day of Pentecost He was sent to earth to live within us and be our Comforter. Let's look at the biblical account.

Nevertheless I tell you the truth; It is expedient for you that I go away: for if I go not away, the Comforter will not come unto you; but if I depart, I will send him unto you.

John 16:7

And, being assembled together with them, (Jesus) commanded them that they should not depart from Jerusalem, but wait for the promise of the Father, which, saith he, ye have heard of me.

For John truly baptized with water; but ye shall be baptized with the Holy Ghost not many days hence.

Acts 1:4,5

The Old Testament prophet Joel said these words:

And it shall come to pass in the last days, saith God, I will pour out of my Spirit upon all flesh....

Acts 2:16,17

• Is the Holy Spirit still around today?

The truth is that the Holy Spirit is here for *all time!* He was here on earth **in the beginning** (Gen. 1:1,2), and He is here today. Remember, Jesus and the Holy Spirit are really One in the Trinity.

So what does the Bible tell us about Jesus?

Jesus Christ the same yesterday, and today, and for ever.

Hebrews 13:8

There are a multitude of Scriptures implying that the Holy Spirit is still with us, but there are no Scriptures telling us He ever went away! The Holy Spirit has been around since the beginning, and continues to be with us.

Jesus said:

Nevertheless I tell you the truth; It is expedient for you that I go away: for if I go not away, the Comforter will not come unto you; but if I depart, I will send him unto you.

John 16:7

The apostle Peter referred to the promise of the Holy Spirit in this manner:

For the promise is unto you, and to your children, and to all that are afar off, even as many as the Lord our God shall call.

Acts 2:39

This means the Holy Spirit was sent here to everyone, for all time!

When God sent Jesus to earth, He gave us another Source upon which to rely. He provided Someone Who could understand our problems and serve as the Sacrifice for all mankind. Likewise, when Jesus left the earth, He did not leave us alone. That's why He said:

And I will pray the Father, and he shall give you another Comforter, that he may abide with you for ever;

Even the Spirit of truth; whom the world cannot receive, because it seeth him not, neither knoweth him: but ye know him; for he dwelleth with you, and shall be in you.

I will not leave you comfortless: I will come to you.

John 14:16-18

- ## Where is the Holy Spirit now?

Not only is the Holy Spirit everywhere God is, but it may surprise you to find that He is inside you; that is, if you are a born-again believer in Christ. He dwells in each and every believer.

That's awesome, but then that's just like our God! He is such an individual God.

It makes sense then that He would send the Holy Spirit to dwell within each believer and minister to us on a one-to-one basis. Here are a number of Scriptures giving support to the fact that the Holy Spirit lives within us:

> **Even the Spirit of truth; whom the world cannot receive, because it seeth him not, neither knoweth him: but ye know him; for he dwelleth with you, and shall be in you.**
>
> **John 14:17**

> **But if the Spirit of him that raised up Jesus from the dead dwell in you, he that raised up Christ from the dead shall also quicken your mortal bodies by his Spirit that dwelleth in you.**
>
> **Romans 8:11**

> **Know ye not that ye are the temple of God, and that the Spirit of God dwelleth in you?**
>
> **1 Corinthians 3:16**

> **That good thing which was committed unto thee keep by the Holy Ghost which dwelleth in us.**
>
> **2 Timothy 1:14**

> **Whosoever shall confess that Jesus is the Son of God, God dwelleth in him, and he in God.**
>
> **1 John 4:15**

- ## Why doesn't the world understand the Holy Spirit?

The apostle John tells us in his gospel that the Spirit of Truth (that's the Holy Spirit) cannot be received by the world.

(John 14:17.) Why? Because they have not accepted Jesus as their Lord and Savior.

Jesus is the One Who sent the Holy Spirit to live within us. If you don't accept Jesus, how can you have a relationship with the Holy Spirit? By the same token, if you don't believe in Jesus or His promises, you are still walking in darkness and cannot see or know the Holy Spirit. Fortunately John's gospel continues by saying that we as Christians *do* know Him, and He dwells within us!

> **Even the Spirit of truth; whom the world cannot receive, because it seeth him not, neither knoweth him: but ye know him; for he dwelleth with you, and shall be in you.**
>
> **John 14:17**

- **I believe in God and I believe in Jesus, but I'm not sure about this "Holy Spirit."**

Who gave you a choice? It certainly wasn't God, Jesus or the Bible! The facts are very clear, my friend.

Remember this: God, Jesus and the Holy Spirit are one Entity. These Three make up the Trinity. How can you accept only Two of Them? God did not say it was "the best two out of three." You need the Holy Spirit for the same reason that you need God — and more. You need the Holy Spirit because He helps you understand the things of God.

God has made us promises in His Word, and we should strive to attain them. One of the best gifts He has given us is the Holy Spirit. Can we truly say we have no need of the Spirit of God in our lives? The truth is, not only do we need Him, we should be elated to have the chance to receive Him!

- **Why do I need the Holy Spirit? What is His purpose?**

I'm so glad you asked! It's important that we understand the vital role the Holy Spirit plays in our Christian lives. The purpose of the Holy Spirit is as difficult to explain as the vastness of God. Like God, the Holy Spirit is greater than can be expressed in our human terms.

To help you get a basic understanding of the Holy Spirit, I have set out ten points of description. These points clearly reveal the purpose of the Holy Spirit as shown throughout the Scriptures and our need for Him in our lives.

The Holy Spirit is our Comforter.

A comforter is a friend who will love you in good times and bad. A comforter will help you through the hard times, taking you by the hand and leading you through the darkest hours. The Holy Spirit has been given as our Comforter.

> **And I will pray the Father, and he shall give you another Comforter, that he may abide with you for ever.**
>
> **John 14:16**

> **But the Comforter, which is the Holy Ghost, whom the Father will send in my name, he shall teach you all things, and bring all things to your remembrance, whatsoever I have said unto you.**
>
> **John 14:26**

> **But when the Comforter is come, whom I will send unto you from the Father, even the Spirit of truth, which proceedeth from the Father, he shall testify of me.**
>
> **John 15:26**

> **Nevertheless I tell you the truth; It is expedient for you that I go away: for if I go not away, the Comforter will not come unto you; but if I depart, I will send him unto you.**
>
> **John 16:7**

The Holy Spirit reveals Truth.

The Holy Spirit is the Spirit of Truth. (John 15:26.)

Along with the Father and Jesus, He holds all the Truth of the universe in His hands. The exciting part is: He is willing to share that Truth with us!

> **Even the Spirit of truth; whom the world cannot receive, because it seeth him not, neither knoweth him: but ye know him; for he dwelleth with you, and shall be in you.**
>
> John 14:17

> **But when the Comforter is come, whom I will send unto you from the Father, even the Spirit of truth, which proceedeth from the Father, he shall testify of me.**
>
> John 15:26

> **Howbeit when he, the Spirit of truth, is come, he will guide you into all truth: for he shall not speak of himself; but whatsoever he shall hear, that shall he speak: and he will shew you things to come.**
>
> John 16:13

> **This is he that came by water and blood, even Jesus Christ; not by water only, but by water and blood. And it is the Spirit that beareth witness, because the Spirit is truth.**
>
> 1 John 5:6

Remember, Jesus said the Spirit is the Truth and God's Word is the Truth. (John 14:6; 17:17.) Since the Holy Spirit is the Spirit of Truth, He will most certainly lead you to a new understanding of the deity of Jesus Christ!

Second Corinthians 3:17 says, **Where the Spirit of the Lord is, there is liberty.** It all comes together when you read in John 8:32 where Jesus said, **The truth shall make you free.** The Holy Spirit will lead you to Truth and set you free.

The Holy Spirit teaches us and helps us to remember the Scriptures.

What good would our Helper be if He didn't help us to grow? Another of the Holy Spirit's jobs is to teach us and help us to learn more about God.

> **But the Comforter, which is the Holy Ghost, whom the Father will send in my name, he shall teach you all things, and *bring all things to your remembrance*, whatsoever I have said unto you.**
>
> John 14:26

Other Scriptures about the Holy Spirit are:

> **For the Holy Ghost shall teach you in the same hour what ye ought to say.**
>
> Luke 12:12

> **But God hath revealed them unto us by his Spirit: for the Spirit searcheth all things, yea, the deep things of God.**
>
> 1 Corinthians 2:10

What better Teacher to have than the Holy Spirit? He knows God inside and out!

The Holy Spirit testifies/witnesses about Jesus.

The baptism of the Holy Spirit will open the door to a deeper relationship with Jesus. This is what reveals that we are truly dealing with the Holy Spirit and not some demonic spirit.

The Holy Spirit was sent to help us by revealing Truth as is found in the Scriptures. How could He reveal Truth in the Scriptures without testifying of the deity of Jesus Christ?

Jesus and the Holy Spirit will always testify of each other. They will never disagree or have any conflicting truths regarding the Scriptures and the promises of God.

> **But when the Comforter is come, whom I will send unto you from the Father, even the Spirit of truth, which proceedeth from the Father, he shall testify of me.**
>
> John 15:26

> **Howbeit when he, the Spirit of truth, is come, he will guide you into all truth: for he shall not speak of**

himself; but whatsoever he shall hear, that shall he speak: and he will shew you things to come.

He shall glorify me: for he shall receive of mine, and shall shew it unto you.

All things that the Father hath are mine: therefore said I, that he shall take of mine, and shall shew it unto you.

John 16:13-15

The Holy Spirit provides power!

We have already shown how the Holy Spirit was sent to help us after Jesus left the earth.

Would Jesus give us a Weapon with no bullets?

Would He provide us a Helper that was weak?

Would He send us a Reinforcement that wasn't prepared for battle?

No!

Jesus sent us a powerful Ally, a Helper Who exceeds all others, the very Spirit of God! We are weak in ourselves and we need a powerful Helper, so we have one.

But here's the best part: He lives within us and gives us power through Him!

Let's look at some examples of His Power at work:

Jesus

How God anointed Jesus of Nazareth with the Holy Ghost and with power: who went about doing good, and healing all that were oppressed of the devil; for God was with him.

Acts 10:38

Believers at Pentecost

And, behold, I send the promise of my Father upon you: but tarry ye in the city of Jerusalem, until ye be endued with power from on high.

Luke 24:49

But ye shall receive power, after that the Holy Ghost is come upon you: and ye shall be witnesses unto me both in Jerusalem, and in all Judaea, and in Samaria, and unto the uttermost part of the earth.

Acts 1:8

Stephen

...and they chose Stephen, a man full of faith and of the Holy Ghost....

And Stephen, full of faith and power, did great wonders and miracles among the people.

Acts 6:5,8

Paul

Through mighty signs and wonders, by the power of the Spirit of God; so that from Jerusalem, and round about unto Illyricum, I have fully preached the gospel of Christ.

Romans 15:19

And my speech and my preaching was not with enticing words of man's wisdom, but in demonstration of the Spirit and of power.

1 Corinthians 2:4

For our gospel came not unto you in word only, but also in power, and in the Holy Ghost, and in much assurance; as ye know what manner of men we were among you for your sake.

1 Thessalonians 1:5

Jesus did not begin His earthly ministry until *after* the Holy Spirit came upon Him. His first miracle was not performed until *after* the Holy Spirit came upon Him. Similarly, He told His disciples to wait in Jerusalem until they were **endued with power from on high** (Luke 24:49).

There is no doubt that the Holy Spirit is the Source of that power — the power to witness, the power to perform great things in His Name. This power is to be used for His service.

The Holy Spirit is a down payment on our inheritance.

One purpose of the Holy Spirit in our lives is to give us a little taste of what God has in store for us. The Holy Spirit is *God's Deposit*, His first installment towards our inheritance. He gives us hope to keep on striving towards the goal.

> **Now it is God who makes both us and you stand firm in Christ. He anointed us, set his seal of ownership on us, and put his Spirit in our hearts as a deposit, guaranteeing what is to come.**
>
> **2 Corinthians 1:21,22 (NIV)**

> **Now it is God who has made us for this very purpose and has given us the Spirit as a deposit, guaranteeing what is to come.**
>
> **2 Corinthians 5:5 (NIV)**

> **And you also were included in Christ when you heard the word of truth, the gospel of your salvation. Having believed, you were marked in him with a seal, the promised Holy Spirit, who is a deposit guaranteeing our inheritance until the redemption of those who are God's possession — to the praise of his glory.**
>
> **Ephesians 1:13,14 (NIV)**

I love this last Scripture. We were marked by Him with a Seal, which is the Holy Spirit. He is our "Stamp of Approval" by Jesus! And that Seal guarantees our inheritance that waits with God.

The Holy Spirit intercedes for us.

The Holy Spirit is our Helper! What better help could He give than to help us in our prayers? The Holy Spirit knows the mind and will of the Father, so He can help us in our prayer life to "get the most out of it."

> **Likewise the Spirit also helpeth our infirmities: for we know not what we should pray for as we ought: but the Spirit itself maketh intercession for us with groanings which cannot be uttered.**
>
> **And he that searcheth the hearts knoweth what is the mind of the Spirit, because he maketh intercession for the saints according to the will of God.**
>
> **Romans 8:26,27**

When we reach the point that we've run out of words or don't know how to pray about a need, that's when the Holy Spirit really takes over. He will pray the perfect prayer on our behalf because He knows our innermost desires, and He knows the will of God. It's great to have an inside track!

The Holy Spirit directs us in the will of God.

Another of the important functions of the Holy Spirit is His help in directing our lives.

He will provide direction and guidance for your next step in God's plan for you. The hard part is that you have to ask! The Holy Spirit won't go where He is not wanted. But He will show you His desires for you and those around you if you will submit to Him.

Here are a few biblical examples of the Spirit's leading in men's lives:

Philip and the Eunuch

> **Then the Spirit said unto Philip, Go near, and join thyself to this chariot.**
>
> **Acts 8:29**

Peter and Cornelius

> **While Peter thought on the vision, the Spirit said unto him, Behold, three men seek thee.**
>
> **Acts 10:19**

Barnabas and Paul at Antioch

While they were worshiping the Lord and fasting, the Holy Spirit said, "Set apart for me Barnabas and Saul for the work to which I have called them."

Acts 13:2 (NIV)

Jesus

Even Jesus submitted to the Holy Spirit's leading. Immediately after Jesus was baptized in water and the Holy Spirit had descended upon Him, look what happened:

Then was Jesus led up of the Spirit into the wilderness to be tempted of the devil.

Matthew 4:1

Do you think Jesus *wanted* to be tempted by the devil? Of course not! He was following the guidance of the Holy Spirit. He knew the Holy Spirit would direct Him only in the way of the Father.

The Holy Spirit builds faith.

Without a doubt, the Holy Spirit is truly a Helper in the area of faith. Since He teaches you all Truth, you can begin to see more clearly the promises of God.

The Holy Spirit will be a never-ending Source of information, encouragement and faith building.

And my speech and my preaching was not with enticing words of man's wisdom, but in demonstration of the Spirit and of power:

That your faith should not stand in the wisdom of men, but in the power of God.

1 Corinthians 2:4,5

But ye, beloved, building up yourselves on your most holy faith, praying in the Holy Ghost,

Keep yourselves in the love of God, looking for the mercy of our Lord Jesus Christ unto eternal life.

Jude 20,21

The Holy Spirit convicts and convinces the world of sin.

The Scripture says that the Holy Spirit was sent to **reprove the world of sin** (John 16:8). The word *reprove* means to convince.[1] He was sent to convince us of the Truth. He was sent to open our eyes that we understand the reality of God and the importance of Jesus. He also reveals to us that we are all indeed sinners, which will move us towards repentance.

When He *convicts* us, it is not a harsh, condescending type of conviction; it is a gentle pull on our hearts. It is that soft, still voice of our conscience. The Holy Spirit will gently notify us that we are living out of God's will, and just as gently He will guide us onto the correct path to take us out of danger.

> **Nevertheless I tell you the truth; It is expedient for you that I go away: for if I go not away, the Comforter will not come unto you; but if I depart, I will send him unto you.**
>
> **And when he is come, he will reprove the world of sin, and of righteousness, and of judgment:**
>
> **Of sin, because they believe not on me;**
>
> **Of righteousness, because I go to my Father, and ye see me no more;**
>
> **Of judgment, because the prince of this world is judged.**
>
> **John 16:7-11**

• **How can I believe in something I haven't seen?**

By faith, my friend, by faith! You cannot see the wind, but you know it is there. You sense its presence, and you have seen its power. The same is true with the Holy Spirit. Though He is unseen in the physical realm, He is flowing with great power in the spiritual realm. The Bible says it so clearly:

> **Now faith is the substance of things hoped for, the evidence of things not seen.**
>
> **Hebrews 11:1**

In other words, we have to believe in the Holy Spirit by faith, just like we believe in God and Jesus. (Most of us have never seen Them either.) The Holy Spirit has taken a backseat over the years and is thought of as "some mysterious thing" that you just can't grasp.

Well, I'm here to tell you that He is as real as this book you're reading! He is alive, and He is still doing wonderful things for believers today. Jesus sent Him to minister to us, and He will not quit that job until Jesus returns for us! I cannot say it better than Jesus Himself:

> **Jesus saith unto him, Thomas, because thou hast seen me, thou hast believed: blessed are they that have not seen, and yet have believed.**
>
> **John 20:29**

• **What about "blasphemy of the Holy Spirit"?**

I will be honest with you. No one knows for certain the limits to which we can go without blaspheming the Holy Spirit. All I can give you is my interpretation based on the Scriptures. Here's what the Bible says about it:

> **Wherefore I say unto you, All manner of sin and blasphemy shall be forgiven unto men: but the blasphemy against the Holy Ghost shall not be forgiven unto men.**
>
> **And whosoever speaketh a word against the Son of man, it shall be forgiven him: but whosoever speaketh against the Holy Ghost, it shall not be forgiven him, neither in this world, neither in the world to come.**
>
> **Matthew 12:31,32**

> **Verily I say unto you, All sins shall be forgiven unto the sons of men, and blasphemies wherewith soever they shall blaspheme:**
>
> **But he that shall blaspheme against the Holy Ghost hath never forgiveness, but is in danger of eternal damnation:**
>
> **Because they said, He hath an unclean spirit.**
>
> **Mark 3:28-30**

Notice that both of these Scripture quotations clearly distinguish between Jesus and the Holy Spirit. Again, this is a testimony that the Holy Spirit is a separate and real Entity.

Now let me point out that people who blaspheme due to ignorance are not the ones at which this Scripture is aimed. Those people are simply ignorant of the Holy Spirit, having not accepted Him, and they can be forgiven through God's mercy.

Even those who know about God yet choose to reject Him can be forgiven. This is obviously true because many who have spoken against God and Jesus later became converted. Paul is a prime example.

So what constitutes *blasphemy*?

First, I think we can agree that blasphemy of the Holy Spirit indicates a clear and willful sin against Him. It seems to center around a twisting of the truth regarding the Holy Spirit.

But, more specifically, the Scriptures suggest that this blasphemy involves certain references to the Holy Spirit as "coming from Satan."

> **And the scribes which came down from Jerusalem said, He hath Beelzebub, and by the prince of the devils casteth he out devils.**
>
> **Mark 3:22**

These scribes were teachers of the Law. They were proclaiming that the power behind Jesus was the power of Satan and that Jesus could do those things because He was possessed.

Such words would be an abomination unto God and directly against the Spirit of Truth, which is the Holy Spirit.

It was these scribes' accusations that Jesus' power came from Satan which initiated His statement about the blasphemy of the Holy Spirit.

The Bible states specifically why He made that declaration. It was:

> **Because they said, He hath an unclean spirit.**
>
> **Mark 3:30**

Some people translate these "no forgiveness" references in Matthew 12 and Mark 3 to mean that the sin is unforgivable "as long as you are still in it."

Others say the word *never* means *Never!*

All I know is, wherever that line may be, we *don't* want to cross it!

Remember, we are not talking about words spoken in anger or in a moment of confusion but through a concentrated, willful rejection of the Holy Spirit.

If you believe in God, Jesus and the reality of the Holy Spirit, and live by Their rules, you will not enter into this territory.

If concerned, your best bet is to learn all you can about the Holy Spirit so you will no longer make foolish statements about Him. This book was written for that purpose: to inform, enlighten and encourage you in your search for the truth about the Holy Spirit.

---

[1]James H. Strong, *Strong's Exhaustive Concordance*, Compact ed. (Grand Rapids: Baker, Reprinted 1992), "Greek Dictionary of the New Testament," p. 27, #1651.

2

The Baptism of the Holy Spirit

The primary purpose of this chapter is to introduce you to the *baptism of the Holy Spirit*. This is a new term and a new concept to many readers, so I have decided to invest some time on the concept before discussing the gifts of the Spirit and other aspects of Holy Spirit baptism.

Before we go any further, let me say that the baptism in the Holy Spirit is the key to this entire book.

"The baptism," as it is often called, can be the most exciting event in your life, next to salvation. If you are really seeking to know the mysteries of God, this is where it all begins.

The Holy Spirit is the One Who will help you and teach you the things of God. The baptism in the Holy Spirit is the open invitation for Him to begin.

• **What is the "baptism in the Holy Spirit"?**

First, when you accept Jesus into your life, you automatically get the Holy Spirit too.

> **Whosoever shall confess that Jesus is the Son of God, God dwelleth in him....**
>
> 1 John 4:15

> **Know ye not that ye are the temple of God, and that the Spirit of God dwelleth in you?**
>
> 1 Corinthians 3:16

The baptism *in, of* or *with* the Holy Spirit refers to the supernatural experience in a believer's life — after salvation

— when the Holy Spirit is supernaturally poured out on a believer as the individual releases the Spirit into his life.

> **...in the last days, saith God, I will pour out of my Spirit upon all flesh....**
>
> **Acts 2:17**

John the Baptist was the first to use this term in foretelling the works of Jesus. He said:

> **I indeed have baptized you with water: but he shall baptize you with the Holy Ghost.**
>
> **Mark 1:8**

Later, Jesus also speaks of this baptism. He was not talking about water baptism, because the disciples would already have been baptized in water.

> **But Jesus said unto them, Ye know not what ye ask: can ye drink of the cup that I drink of? and be baptized with the baptism that I am baptized with?**
>
> **And they said unto him, We can. And Jesus said unto them, Ye shall indeed drink of the cup that I drink of; and with the baptism that I am baptized withal shall ye be baptized.**
>
> **Mark 10:38,39**

Jesus was promising His disciples that they would receive the same baptism in the Holy Spirit which He had received.

Then just days before the experience at Pentecost, Jesus Himself reiterated the statement of John the Baptist as He again promised this baptism:

> **For John truly baptized with water; but ye shall be *baptized with the Holy Ghost* not many days hence.**
>
> **Acts 1:5**

Jesus' words **not many days hence** referred to the disciples' experience in Jerusalem. While in the upper room on the day of Pentecost, the disciples and many others (about 120) received the baptism in the Holy Spirit.

> **And they were all filled with the Holy Ghost, and began to speak with other tongues, as the Spirit gave them utterance.**
>
> **Acts 2:4**

Later, when the apostle Peter was ministering at the house of Cornelius, he remembered Jesus' words:

> **And as I began to speak, the Holy Ghost fell on them, as on us at the beginning.**
>
> **Then remembered I the word of the Lord, how that he said, John indeed baptized with water; *but ye shall be baptized with the Holy Ghost.***
>
> **Acts 11:15,16**

This confirms that being **filled with the Holy Ghost**, as in Acts 2:4, is synonymous with being **baptized with the Holy Ghost.**

After receiving Jesus unto salvation, you should follow with baptism in water. This water baptism is performed by water being poured upon the believer or by his being immersed in the water as a sign of his submission to God's Word.

You also receive the Holy Spirit when you accept Jesus. But the Word continues to say you can be baptized (immersed) in the Holy Spirit. This baptism in the Holy Spirit shows submission to Jesus by allowing Him to pour out the Spirit upon you and immerse you in the Holy Spirit.

- **Show me in the Bible a distinct difference between "water" baptism and baptism "in the Holy Spirit."**

The Bible is definitely the right place to start. Many people want to argue from traditions but not from the Bible.

When reading the Scriptures, the differences between these two baptisms are really quite obvious. The distinction is made in several instances in the Bible. But those who are against Holy Spirit baptism seem to overlook these Scriptures. Let's consider a few examples.

John the Baptist

First, let's look at John the Baptist. He was a forerunner of Jesus and, as his name implies, was well known for baptizing new converts in water. If we examined all four of the gospels, we would see John clearly stating a different kind of baptism. He said that he baptized in water, but that another (Jesus) would come and baptize with the Holy Ghost:

> **I indeed baptize you with water unto repentance: but he that cometh after me is mightier than I, whose shoes I am not worthy to bear: he shall baptize you with the Holy Ghost, and with fire.**
>
> **Matthew 3:11**

(See also Mark 1:8; Luke 3:16; John 1:33.)

How's that for evidence? Four disciples confirm it in God's Word, using the very words of John the Baptist!

Still not convinced? How about Jesus for a witness?

Jesus

Here's what He told the disciples:

> **For John truly baptized with water; but ye shall be baptized with the Holy Ghost not many days hence.**
>
> **Acts 1:5**

We know from the Scriptures that Jesus ascended to heaven and later sent the Holy Ghost on the day of Pentecost. The Bible testifies how on that day the believers in the upper room were baptized in the Holy Spirit and spoke in tongues.

Peter and Cornelius

Another Scripture that clearly shows the distinction between water baptism and Holy Spirit baptism is the story of Peter and Cornelius.

As the Scriptures relate, the apostle Peter went to visit a man named Cornelius in the city of Caesarea. This event was significant because Cornelius was the first Gentile to be offered the Gospel of Jesus Christ. When Peter spoke to those who had gathered there, notice the sequence of events which followed:

> **While Peter yet spake these words, the Holy Ghost fell on all them which heard the word.**
>
> **And they of the circumcision which believed were astonished, as many as came with Peter, because that on the Gentiles also was poured out the gift of the Holy Ghost.**
>
> **For they heard them speak with tongues, and magnify God. Then answered Peter,**
>
> **Can any man forbid water, that these should not be baptized, which have received the Holy Ghost as well as we?**
>
> **And he commanded them to be baptized in the name of the Lord....**
>
> **Acts 10:44-48**

This *pouring out* of the Holy Ghost is synonymous with the baptism in the Holy Spirit and was confirmed by the evidence of speaking in tongues! (We will discuss this *evidence* in the next chapter.)

Then notice how after those believers received Holy Spirit baptism Peter made a special command to have all of them baptized in water.

If the baptism in the Holy Spirit was the same as water baptism, do you think Peter would have made that statement? Of course not!

These are separate and distinct baptisms. In fact, those people had obviously not been baptized in water because they were Gentiles. Until that time, the Gentiles were not even allowed to partake in the Gospel.

Later, as Peter repeats his testimony to the believers in Jerusalem, he remembers Jesus' words:

> **And as I began to speak, the Holy Ghost fell on them, as on us at the beginning.**

Then remembered I the word of the Lord, how that
he said, John indeed baptized with water; but ye shall
be baptized with the Holy Ghost.

Acts 11:15,16

Paul and the Ephesians

How about another example? Let's look at the story of the
apostle Paul with the believers at Ephesus:

And it came to pass, that, while Apollos was at
Corinth, Paul having passed through the upper coasts
came to Ephesus: and finding certain disciples,

He said unto them, Have ye received the Holy
Ghost since ye believed? And they said unto him, We
have not so much as heard whether there be any Holy
Ghost.

And he said unto them, Unto what then were ye
baptized? And they said, Unto John's baptism.

Then said Paul, John verily baptized with the
baptism of repentance, saying unto the people, that
they should believe on him which should come after
him, that is, on Christ Jesus.

When they heard this, they were baptized in the
name of the Lord Jesus.

And when Paul had laid his hands upon them, the
Holy Ghost came on them; and they spake with
tongues, and prophesied.

Acts 19:1-6

Again, we see clear indication of a separation between
these two baptisms. Paul specifically asked if they had
received the (baptism in the) Holy Ghost. They said they
never even heard of the Holy Ghost (or the baptism), that they
had received only John's baptism (or water baptism).

After Paul heard this, he did not stop and say, "Well, that's
enough." No! He laid hands on them that they might receive
Holy Spirit baptism.

As you can clearly see, the Bible gives us ample confirmation that there is a distinction between water baptism and Holy Spirit baptism. Of course, each of these has its own importance, and neither is to be belittled.

My intent is to show that there are indeed two separate events of baptism which the Lord desires us to receive. There is, however, undeniably a parallel between these baptisms.

Water baptism requires that believers be immersed in water as a sign of their submission to God and His Word. Holy Spirit baptism shows believers' submission to Jesus by allowing Him to pour out His Spirit upon them, immersing them in the Holy Spirit.

Both types of baptism require obedience and faith on the part of the believer. Each baptism has but one requirement: you must accept Jesus as your Savior. Then there are three key ingredients:

1. Someone to perform the baptism
2. Some substance with which to be baptized
3. A candidate willing to receive

Water baptism requires a minister, some water and you.

Holy Spirit baptism requires Jesus, the Holy Spirit and you.

Our God has a wonderfully orchestrated plan for His children. By faith we take action to request both baptisms, then we must submit to the baptizer. In either case, to be baptized we must stop running around trying to receive and simply submit. We must act in faith, being obedient to the Lord in each step of submission:

1. Accepting Jesus shows submission to God.
2. Being baptized in water shows submission to Jesus.
3. Being baptized in the Holy Spirit shows submission to the Holy Spirit (and to Jesus).

- **Can you better explain "receiving" the baptism?**

A pastor friend once gave me a good analogy. I'll share it with you.

Let's say a friend comes to visit you at your home. When he knocks at the door, you are busy in another room, so you yell out, "Come in!" Your friend then comes inside your home, but you still haven't "received" him. Everyone can agree he has arrived, and he even feels welcome in your home. But he has not yet had the fellowship for which he came. Until you actually go to him and greet him, you have not really received him into your home. (Of course, if he were unwanted, the opposite action would be to reject him.)

When it comes to the Holy Spirit, most people tend to be somewhere in the middle. They don't reject Him and they don't receive Him; they simply ignore Him. (Hint: Ignoring is the same as rejecting.)

Here's another analogy:

Suppose you and I are best friends. When your birthday is approaching, I naturally want to give you a gift, so I search to find the perfect gift. When that day arrives, I bring the gift to your house and set it on the table by your birthday cake.

I am excited for you to open the gift, because I just know you will love it! But the final decision to receive that gift is yours. You may choose to immediately unwrap it and receive it with great joy. Or you could leave it laying there, always wondering what's inside. It is your choice.

For some reason — maybe pride, fear of disappointment, or some other concern — you don't open that gift. Instead, you decide to simply carry it around with you everywhere you go.

There's no arguing that you have the gift. You possess it. But you have never received it for everything it was intended. You haven't received all the joy it can give you. Neither have you allowed me, the giver, to be blessed by receiving my gift and recognizing my love for you. Have you forgotten that I'm your best friend? I know you better than anyone, and I would be giving you something really special!

This is what we do to Jesus with the Holy Spirit. He gives us that incredible Gift for our joy and benefit. But we just let that Gift sit there. We don't receive Him because of pride, fear, stubbornness, tradition or some other reason. We carry Him around inside of us, never bothering to receive Him as our personal Friend. The wonderful part is that once we have received Him there is still just as much of Him available for everyone else!

This whole concept of *receiving* seems to hinder many believers from being baptized in the Holy Spirit. The problem really boils down to their trying to logically explain supernatural things from God.

Sometimes it's difficult to explain God's supernatural works because of our limited understanding. Our earthly definitions aren't always sufficient.

Maybe looking at this question from a different angle will help you to understand.

Releasing

Rather than thinking of *receiving* the Holy Spirit, think of it as *releasing* the Holy Spirit.

You are releasing the Spirit and His power to flow through you.

You are saying to the Lord, "I want to receive the Holy Spirit and all He has for me. I want You to use me in whatever way is pleasing to You, Lord."

Think of it like a carbonated soft drink. The power (fizz) resides within the container but does not become evident until we do something: shake it up. There is no argument that the power was always present, but there is no release until we shake it up and then open the top!

The Holy Spirit works the same within us. He lives within us in mighty power, but until we make a move to receive Him, we will remain "flat." First, we must ask for the baptism, which will shake us out of our normal state; then we must open ourselves and see the Holy Spirit pour forth in power!

As you release the Holy Spirit of God, Jesus will baptize you (submerge you) in His Holy Spirit. Like that soft drink, when the power flows forth, you can't help but get wet!

The bottom line is this: we are not called to understand *every* aspect of Holy Spirit baptism; we *are* called to obey His Word and accept it in humbleness and faith.

- **I "received" the Holy Spirit when I got saved. Why should I receive Him again?**

Let me repeat that the baptism in the Holy Spirit is a separate and distinct event from your initial encounter with the Holy Spirit through salvation.

True, the Holy Spirit did come into your life when you accepted Jesus Christ as your Savior.

True, accepting Jesus as your Savior is all that is required of salvation.

True, the love, joy, peace and other spiritual forces you have experienced since being saved are from the Holy Spirit.

But what we are really talking about receiving is the *baptism in* the Holy Spirit. This experience occurs *after* salvation. Consider it an upgrade or a booster! Jesus wants to make our time here on earth even more exciting as believers. He wants to build on that love and joy we have received. He wants to add power, boldness and excitement!

On the day of Jesus' ascension to heaven, the disciples could have made the same statements of faith that we just discussed. They had everything they needed to get to heaven. But Jesus *still* commanded them to go to Jerusalem and wait for the baptism of the Holy Spirit.

Let's look again at the apostle Paul's experience with the Ephesians:

> **And it came to pass, that, while Apollos was at Corinth, Paul having passed through the upper coasts came to Ephesus: and finding certain disciples,**
>
> **He said unto them, Have ye received the Holy Ghost since ye believed? And they said unto him, We have not so much as heard whether there be any Holy Ghost.**
>
> **Acts 19:1,2**

Notice this says that Paul met **certain disciples**. So these people were already believers who had accepted Christ. Then he asked them, **Have ye received the Holy Ghost *since ye believed*?**

Don't you think Paul knew about the Holy Spirit coming to live inside the believers when they had accepted Christ? Of course he did.

It's also obvious that he knew they had made a commitment to Christ, because he used the words **since ye believed**. Why would he ask whether they had received the Holy Ghost if there was nothing left for them to receive? The answer is simple: he wanted them to receive *the baptism* in the Holy Ghost!

So then what happened? See for yourself:

> **And when Paul had laid his hands upon them, the Holy Ghost came on them; and they spake with tongues, and prophesied.**
>
> **Acts 19:6**

The Bible clearly shows that the baptism in the Holy Spirit is separate from salvation. The Scriptures which we cited previously give additional support to this:

Acts 2:33,38	Peter and disciples at Pentecost
Acts 8:14-19	Peter, John, Simon and Samaritans
Acts 10:44-48	Peter and Cornelius
Acts 4:31	Peter describing believers in Early Church at Jerusalem
Acts 9:17,18	Paul and Ananias

- **How can I receive something I already have?**

I understand your question. If you are a Christian, you already have the Holy Spirit living inside you. Then you naturally question the value of asking for something you already possess.

Again, let me make a clarification. Having the Holy Spirit does *not* mean you have received the *baptism in* the Holy

Spirit, just like having a baptismal full of water does not mean you have been water baptized.

My point is this: it is the action, not the element, which produces the results. Even though you *receive* water, in the sense that you are submersed into it, it's not the water that is significant; it's the action!

Being baptized in water is an act of obedience. There is never a question that water is for use in the baptism, but you are still not baptized until you ask to be baptized in it.

The same is true for being baptized in the Holy Spirit. You must ask Jesus to baptize you, so that you may receive the baptism in the Holy Spirit.

- **My church believes in a "second act of grace," or "second blessing." Is this the same as the baptism of the Holy Spirit?**

It depends. This means different things to different churches, but often it does refer to the baptism of the Holy Spirit.

However, some churches when using these terms purposefully omit some of the spiritual gifts. This varies with denominations. While some choose to ignore *all* gifts, others omit *only* the gifts of speaking in tongues and interpretation of tongues.

Scripturally speaking, this practice does not follow the biblical pattern, nor is there any support for picking and choosing only those gifts you want.

As for the terms themselves, such as *second act of grace*, I have no problem with these terms per se. The baptism is without a doubt given by grace just as all of God's promises are.

My concern is that in some cases this is simply an attempt to gloss over the phrase *baptism in the Holy Ghost* to avoid controversy. Although this is how the Bible refers to the experience, this term stirs up strong emotions in many people because of their rejection to the whole "tongues issue."

For this reason, some denominations use softer words like *second blessing* to tone down the more controversial issue of "baptism in the Holy Spirit."

For John truly baptized with water; but ye shall be baptized with the Holy Ghost not many days hence.

Acts 1:5

Please understand that in no way am I belittling these people's experiences. In many cases they are experiencing the fullness of the baptism of the Holy Spirit.

The terminology used is not as important as the teaching surrounding this subject. The important thing is how people are receiving God's promise of the baptism of the Holy Spirit and all the gifts that are available to them.

I am simply directing your attention to the sometimes subtle differences in beliefs. The Lord expects us to check every teaching against His Word to ensure that the Truth is being taught.

- **What is meant by the phrase, "Spirit Filled"?**

The term *Spirit Filled* is taken from the many Scripture verses referring to an infilling (or baptism) of the Holy Ghost.

And they were all filled with the Holy Ghost, and began to speak with other tongues, as the Spirit gave them utterance.

Acts 2:4

(See also Luke 1:41,67; Acts 4:8,31; 9:17; 13:9,52; Eph. 5:18.)

- **Were the disciples baptized in the Holy Spirit while walking with Jesus?**

Not before Jesus had died on the cross; that wasn't God's plan!

The disciples were walking and talking with God in the flesh: Jesus *was* God! They were eating, drinking, learning, sharing and following Jesus every day.

It wasn't until *after* Jesus left the earth that the disciples truly needed a new Helper. Jesus told them that the Spirit would be given to them *after* He (Jesus) was glorified:

> **He that believeth on me, as the scripture hath said, out of his belly shall flow rivers of living water.**
>
> **(But this spake he of the Spirit, which they that believe on him should receive: for the Holy Ghost was not yet given; because that Jesus was not yet glorified.)**
>
> **John 7:38,39**

The disciples were chosen during a transition time between the Savior being sent and the Holy Spirit being sent. During that time the Holy Spirit was still being poured out on specific people for specific functions, just like in the Old Testament. He had not yet been given to all mankind.

Notice what Jesus said regarding the Holy Spirit:

> **Even the Spirit of truth; whom the world cannot receive, because it seeth him not, neither knoweth him: but ye know him; for he dwelleth with you, and shall be in you.**
>
> **John 14:17**

Jesus said to the disciples that the Holy Spirit **dwelleth** *with* **you, and shall be** *in* **you.** At that time the Holy Spirit was *with* them because they were with Jesus and doing God's work. But He said that in the near future the Holy Spirit would be *in* them.

Jesus was, of course, referring to the day of Pentecost. On that day the Holy Spirit came to reside in every born-again believer for all time.

• **Did the disciples ever receive the baptism in the Holy Spirit?**

Certainly they did. The Bible clearly shows evidence of this fact. They were baptized in the Holy Spirit at the same time. They all (except for Judas Iscariot) were in the upper room on the day of Pentecost when the Holy Spirit came upon them.

We can see this sequence of events in Scripture. First, Jesus told them to go and wait in Jerusalem:

> **And, being assembled together with them, commanded them that they should not depart from Jerusalem, but wait for the promise of the Father, which, saith he, ye have heard of me.**
>
> **For John truly baptized with water; but ye shall be baptized with the Holy Ghost not many days hence.**
>
> Acts 1:4,5

So they entered Jerusalem and gathered together in an upper room:

> **Then returned they unto Jerusalem from the mount called Olivet, which is from Jerusalem a sabbath day's journey.**
>
> **And when they were come in, they went up into an upper room, where abode both Peter, and James, and John, and Andrew, Philip, and Thomas, Bartholomew, and Matthew, James the son of Alphaeus, and Simon Zelotes, and Judas the brother of James.**
>
> **These all continued with one accord in prayer and supplication, with the women, and Mary the mother of Jesus, and with his brethren.**
>
> **And in those days Peter stood up in the midst of the disciples, and said, (the number of names together were about an hundred and twenty,)....**
>
> Acts 1:12-15

Also, Matthias, who replaced Judas, was present. (Acts 1:26.)

When the Holy Ghost descended upon them, they *all* were filled with the Spirit:

> **And they were all filled with the Holy Ghost, and began to speak with other tongues, as the Spirit gave them utterance.**
>
> Acts 2:4

How much more evidence do we need to believe that the disciples were Spirit filled?

The Bible names them individually!

> **And the disciples were filled with joy, and with the Holy Ghost.**
>
> Acts 13:52

• **If the disciples did not receive the Holy Spirit until Pentecost, why had Jesus already said to them, "Receive ye the Holy Ghost"?**

On one of the occasions in which Jesus appeared to the disciples after the Resurrection, He made the following statements:

> **Then said Jesus to them again, Peace be unto you: as my Father hath sent me, even so send I you.**
> **And when he had said this, he breathed on them, and saith unto them, Receive ye the Holy Ghost.**
>
> John 20:21,22

There are a number of different interpretations of this Scripture. Some think it was simply a symbolic transfer of power and authority to His disciples. Others think that a measure of the Holy Spirit was given to them in preparation for Pentecost.

My personal opinion is that this was when the disciples received their salvation — when they were born again.

You may ask, "Weren't the disciples already saved?"

Remember, none of us received salvation until *after* Jesus had died on the cross. True, the disciples had been walking with Him all that time, but He had not yet gone to the cross. The event we are discussing occurred *after* He was resurrected.

It seems appropriate that Jesus would give them the opportunity to officially receive their salvation. Not the baptism of the Holy Spirit, but the Holy Spirit coming to live within them just as He does in each of us when we are born again.

Please don't confuse this with receiving the baptism of the Holy Spirit. Without a doubt, that did not happen to the disciples until the day of Pentecost. The biblical support for this comes from Jesus Himself. He told the disciples to go to Jerusalem and wait to be endued with power from on high. (Luke 24:49.)

Why would He tell them that if He had already given them the power? Also, Jesus said the Holy Spirit would not come until *after* He had gone to be with the Father. Since He had not yet ascended into heaven, this would be contrary to His own promise.

- **Were there other Spirit-filled men and women in the Bible?**

Many more! Including the disciples, there were 120 people in the upper room. Since the Bible says that *all* were filled, that includes the rest of those 120!

In Acts, chapter 1, we find the following people specifically named:

Mary, mother of Jesus	Acts 1:14
Jesus' brothers	Acts 1:14
Barsabas	Acts 1:23
*Other women	Acts 1:14

Most likely included Mary Magdalene; Joanna; Mary, mother of James and Joseph; and Salome.

* These women were always with Mary. (See also Matt. 27:56; Mark 15:40,47; 16:1; Luke 24:10; John 19:25.)

But these are not the only ones. Elsewhere in the Bible, Scripture confirms that several well-known individuals were Spirit filled. The following are a few of them:

John the Baptist	Luke 1:13-15
Elisabeth, John's mother	Luke 1:41
Zacharias, John's father	Luke 1:67
Stephen	Acts 6:5
Barnabas	Acts 11:22-24
Paul	1 Corinthians 14:18; Acts 13:9
Timothy	2 Timothy 1:6

•How could John the Baptist be filled with the Spirit when Jesus hadn't even been born?

An interesting observation!

Jesus sent the Holy Spirit to minister to us in His absence. But years before that, the Scriptures record how John the Baptist was filled with the Spirit while still in his mother's womb:

> **But the angel said unto him, Fear not, Zacharias: for thy prayer is heard; and thy wife Elisabeth shall bear thee a son, and thou shalt call his name John.**
>
> **And thou shalt have joy and gladness; and many shall rejoice at his birth.**
>
> **For he shall be great in the sight of the Lord, and shall drink neither wine nor strong drink;** *and he shall be filled with the Holy Ghost, even from his mother's womb.*
>
> **Luke 1:13-15**

Since John was a little older than Jesus, how could he have been Spirit filled?

Since the beginning of mankind, God has poured out the Holy Spirit on special people at special times for special tasks. A few examples of this would be Samson, David, Moses and Samuel. Before Jesus came to earth, God dealt directly with His people and, in turn, gave them power through the Holy Spirit. So John was filled with the Spirit under that old system.

Only *after* Jesus returned to the Father was the baptism of the Holy Spirit available to everyone who received Him. Just as Jesus was our final Sacrifice and our Savior, the Holy Spirit was sent as our final Helper.

Since God had a plan for John to witness about the coming of Jesus, He endowed John with power from the Holy Spirit, even while he was in the womb. There wasn't time to waste since John was only a few months older than Jesus! He had to prepare the way!

• Does the Bible support the "baptism in the Holy Spirit"?

Without a doubt!

As we have already shown, there are many, many Scriptures supporting the truth of the baptism in the Holy Spirit. And according to the Bible:

All scripture is given by inspiration of God....
2 Timothy 3:16

If we believe the Bible is truly the inspired Word of God, this leads us to a very interesting conclusion. If you examine the writers of the entire New Testament, you will find that, with the exception of Mark and Luke (the Scriptures do not specify either way), they *all* were baptized in the Holy Spirit.

The following chart shows all of the New Testament authors:

The New Testament

BOOK	ACCEPTED AUTHOR	BOOK	ACCEPTED AUTHOR
Matthew	Matthew	1 Timothy	Paul
Mark	Mark	2 Timothy	Paul
Luke	Luke	Titus	Paul
John	John	Philemon	Paul
Acts	Paul	Hebrews	Paul
Romans	Paul	James	*James
1 Corinthians	Paul	1 Peter	Peter
2 Corinthians	Paul	2 Peter	Peter
Galatians	Paul	1 John	John
Ephesians	Paul	2 John	John
Philippians	Paul	3 John	John
Colossians	Paul	Jude	*Jude
1 Thessalonians	Paul	Revelation	John
2 Thessalonians	Paul		

* These were Jesus' brothers, not the apostles. (See Matthew 13:55; Mark 6:3.)

- **Why is this such a recent event? If it's "of God," why has it only come into play during recent years?**

It's not a "recent event" at all. The disciples received the baptism almost 2,000 years ago! When they received the Holy Spirit at Pentecost, it was a direct fulfillment of Old Testament prophecy:

> **And it shall come to pass afterward, that I will pour out my spirit upon all flesh; and your sons and your daughters shall prophesy, your old men shall dream dreams, your young men shall see visions.**
>
> **Joel 2:28**

> **...I will pour my spirit upon thy seed, and my blessing upon thine offspring.**
>
> **Isaiah 44:3**

Once the Holy Spirit was poured out on mankind, He never left! This is the *same* Holy Spirit, the *same* baptism, the *same* experience which the disciples had.

Through all these years, man has gone through so many religious changes, and for many years the Church was dead in a sense because there was no power. Then around the turn of the century (1900 A.D.), there was a revival of the Holy Ghost. This excitement has spread through all the major denominations.

To sum it up, the reason it seems to have only come about in recent years is because we are finally asking! For so many years the Church was tied up in denominational lines. People seemed always to get caught up in being religious, and they had lost sight of *why* we started religion: because of God!

- **Should I seek the baptism in the Holy Spirit?**

Definitely! If you have accepted Jesus as your Savior, then you are ready to move into the next promise God has for you. If you really desire to receive everything He has for you, you should begin seeking the baptism in the Holy Spirit. Jesus said:

> **...how much more shall your heavenly Father give the Holy Spirit to them that ask him?**
>
> **Luke 11:13**

Notice the key word Jesus used here: **ask**. If you are ready to receive, you must ask Jesus to baptize you in the Holy Spirit. When you seek His promises, He will always be faithful to fulfill them.

3

Tongues: The Sign of Holy Spirit Baptism

Many readers have opened this book and turned immediately to this chapter. How do I know? Simply because of its subject: *speaking in tongues*.

Tongues is by far the most intriguing of all the issues surrounding the baptism in the Holy Spirit. Why? Well, for starters, it's unusual, it's supernatural, and everyone has heard stories about it!

My intent in this chapter is not to single out speaking in tongues as the most important aspect of Holy Spirit baptism, but merely to concentrate on this one aspect which prompts so many questions. I will provide answers to many of the most common questions about tongues.

Before we begin, would you do me a favor? If you haven't read the first two chapters, please read them before going any further. I wouldn't ask this if I did not think it important. The basic information included in chapters 1 and 2 will help you to better understand some of the questions and answers contained in this chapter.

- **What is "speaking in tongues"?**

Specifically, speaking in tongues is a manifestation of the Holy Spirit in a believer (after receiving the baptism in the Holy Spirit), which allows that individual to pray in an unknown language. The purpose of this language is to communicate and fellowship with God.

There are many biblical references to this experience in the book of Acts, which we will discuss later in this chapter.

The Bible clearly gives evidence of tongues as the sign of the baptism in the Holy Spirit. Also, in the book of First Corinthians, tongues is revealed as one of the nine spiritual *gifts*. (The *gift of speaking in tongues* will be covered in a following chapter on the spiritual gifts.)

In this chapter we will concentrate on speaking in tongues as the sign of the baptism.

The Sign of the Baptism of the Holy Spirit

It's important that we learn about tongues because Jesus said this sign will follow His people:

> **And these signs shall follow them that believe; In my name shall they cast out devils; they shall speak with new tongues;**
> **...they shall lay hands on the sick, and they shall recover.**
>
> **Mark 16:17,18**

Some will argue that speaking with new tongues only means that after our salvation we will talk nicer or be more loving. Although this behavior should indeed be the result of walking a Christian walk, that is not what the Bible means by speaking with tongues.

Notice Jesus said, **These *signs* shall follow them that believe.** Just talking nice is not a sign. Lots of people who talk nice can still go straight to hell! It's more than that.

Look at the other signs Jesus mentioned in these two Scripture verses: healing and casting out devils. These are not things you would confuse with activities of the unsaved. They are supernatural signs showing the power of God to unbelievers!

A Prayer Language or Praying in the Spirit

Since speaking in tongues is used in a person's individual prayer life, it is sometimes referred to as a *prayer language* or *praying in the Spirit*.

Tongues is a special spiritual language that God has chosen just for you. You use this unknown tongue for your own personal communication with God!

Speaking in tongues is not always a specific prayer; it can simply be words of praise, thanksgiving, blessing or worship. Tongues is also used for intercession or often for praying about the unknown.

Glossolalia

Occasionally, you will hear the term *glossolalia* when referring to speaking in tongues.

The word *glossolalia* is derived from the Greek word *glossa*, meaning tongue or language.[1] In short, this is the technical word for speaking in tongues.

Other Tongues

There are various terms in the Bible associated with speaking in tongues:

new tongues (Mark 16:17)

other tongues (Acts 2:4)

divers kinds of tongues (1 Cor. 12:10)

an unknown tongue (1 Cor. 14:2)

These are simply different ways of expressing the same subject.

- **What does the Bible mean by "praying with the Spirit and with understanding"?**

Basically, this means praying in tongues but also in the language you normally speak, your conversational language. There should be balance in your prayer life.

> ...I will pray with the spirit, and I will pray with the understanding also: I will sing with the spirit, and I will sing with the understanding also.
>
> **1 Corinthians 14:15**

When you pray in tongues, you are really letting the Holy Spirit do much of the work. But you should also pray in your own language.

There are a couple of reasons for this. First, it shows discipline in your life to actually pray on your own without relying on the Spirit to do all the praying. Second, by praying in your own language, you are speaking words of faith into your own ears.

So then faith cometh by hearing, and hearing by the word of God.

Romans 10:17

The difference between praying in the Spirit and with understanding is something like this:

When you pray through your mind, every word and thought are analyzed before being spoken out. Your heartfelt prayer is sent through your mind to be checked for things like logic, sentence structure and word choice. This can cause you to change your mind or change words in mid-sentence. By the time you speak it forth, it has lost much of the feeling it first had.

When you pray in the Spirit, you bypass your mind. The Holy Spirit goes past all of those self-checking devices in your mind and prays with a fervor, revealing the peace, emotion and submission that can only be experienced.

- **How do we know that tongues is the initial sign of the baptism?**

My first instinct is to answer you by saying, "Because that's just the way it always works!" But rather than go on experience, let's look at some biblical evidence.

The Day of Pentecost

And when the day of Pentecost was fully come, they were all with one accord in one place.

And suddenly there came a sound from heaven as of a rushing mighty wind, and it filled all the house where they were sitting.

> **And there appeared unto them cloven tongues like as of fire, and it sat upon each of them.**
>
> **And they were all filled with the Holy Ghost, and began to speak with other tongues, as the Spirit gave them utterance.**
>
> **Acts 2:1-4**

As foretold by Jesus just before He left the earth, the disciples in Jerusalem were **endued with power from on high** (Luke 24:49). As the Scripture above clearly states *all* 120 of them spoke in tongues **as the Spirit gave them utterance.** The word *utterance* here simply means that the Spirit gave them the words to say in that unknown language.

Peter and the House of Cornelius

Cornelius was told by an angel to seek out Peter, and Peter was told by the Holy Spirit that Cornelius's men were looking for him. So, in obedience, Peter went to the house of Cornelius. While he was preaching to them about the deity of Jesus, this is what happened:

> **While Peter yet spake these words, the Holy Ghost fell on all them which heard the word.**
>
> **And they of the circumcision which believed were astonished, as many as came with Peter, because that on the Gentiles also was poured out the gift of the Holy Ghost.**
>
> **For they heard them speak with tongues, and magnify God....**
>
> **Acts 10:44-46**

Notice that, first, **the Holy Ghost fell on all them**, and then **they heard them speak with tongues**. It even records this as the "pouring out" of the gift of the Holy Ghost.

What happened when they spoke in tongues? They magnified God! Not just some of them but all who heard the Word.

This also testifies that tongues is from God. Whenever the Holy Spirit is present, He will magnify God.

Paul and the Believers at Ephesus

The apostle Paul came to the city of Ephesus and found other believers there. As they shared about their faith, he found out some interesting things:

> He said unto them, Have ye received the Holy Ghost since ye believed? And they said unto him, We have not so much as heard whether there be any Holy Ghost.
>
> And he said unto them, Unto what then were ye baptized? And they said, Unto John's baptism.
>
> Then said Paul, John verily baptized with the baptism of repentance, saying unto the people, that they should believe on him which should come after him, that is, on Christ Jesus.
>
> When they heard this, they were baptized in the name of the Lord Jesus.
>
> And when Paul had laid his hands upon them, the Holy Ghost came on them; and they spake with tongues, and prophesied.
>
> And all the men were about twelve.
>
> Acts 19:2-7

There are some wonderful truths in this passage of Scripture. First, when Paul asked if they had received the baptism of the Holy Spirit, they said, "We've never even heard of such a thing!"

This one simple statement encompasses the thoughts of so many Christians today. I know — I was one of them! When first introduced to the baptism of the Holy Spirit, I had to say, "I've never even heard of it before!"

Lack of information, traditions and stubbornness have kept this wonderful Truth hidden from so many of our Christian friends.

That, my friend, is why I have written this book. I want everyone to know that there is a beautiful promise from God available to any Christian who asks.

Anyway, back to Paul and the Ephesians...

Paul asked them, "Then what baptism did you receive?" They, of course, answered, "John's baptism," meaning water baptism. (This was the primary thing for which John the Baptist had been known.) Then the Scripture says they all were baptized (in water) in the name of Jesus Christ.

Finally, as Paul laid his hands upon them, they received the baptism in the Holy Spirit. How do I know? Because the Scripture says, first, **the Holy Ghost came on them**, and, second, **they spake with tongues.**

Tongues is the sign of the baptism of the Holy Spirit.

Peter, John and the Samaritan Believers

Now when the apostles which were at Jerusalem heard that Samaria had received the word of God, they sent unto them Peter and John:

Who, when they were come down, prayed for them, that they might receive the Holy Ghost:

(For as yet he was fallen upon none of them: only they were baptized in the name of the Lord Jesus.)

Then laid they their hands on them, and they received the Holy Ghost.

And when Simon saw that through laying on of the apostles' hands the Holy Ghost was given, he offered them money,

Saying, Give me also this power, that on whomsoever I lay hands, he may receive the Holy Ghost.

Acts 8:14-19

Let's look at the facts of this event. First, it says Peter and John **prayed for them, that they might** *receive the Holy Ghost.* Then it says the apostles **laid...their hands on them, and they** *received the Holy Ghost.* "Receiving the Holy Ghost" refers to receiving the baptism in the Holy Ghost.

Although tongues is not specifically mentioned in the Samaritans' story, we can read between the lines.

Why was Simon so excited about the Holy Spirit? There was obviously some sign that these believers had received.

Otherwise, how would Peter, John and especially Simon have known it?

Simon would not have been fooled by some type of trickery. He was a sorcerer, and he knew the real thing when he saw it. That's why he wanted it so badly, because it was so remarkable. And he wanted the power too!

Like all other biblical references, the sign must have been speaking in tongues.

Paul and Ananias

And Ananias went his way, and entered into the house; and putting his hands on him said, Brother Saul (or Paul), **the Lord, even Jesus, that appeared unto thee in the way as thou camest, hath sent me, that thou mightest receive thy sight, and be filled with the Holy Ghost.**

And immediately there fell from his eyes as it had been scales: and he received sight forthwith, and arose, and was baptized.

Acts 9:17,18

Ananias was sent on a mission from the Lord. What was his mission? He told Saul (Paul) that Jesus had sent him **that thou mightest receive thy sight,** *and* **be filled with the Holy Ghost.** He had been sent on a two-part mission, if you will.

Then the Scripture says that when the scales fell from Saul's eyes he **arose, and was baptized.** Perhaps he was water baptized, but he was definitely baptized in the Holy Spirit!

How can we be sure of this? For one thing, it is the second of the two tasks Jesus had given to Ananias. Do you think that Ananias, if working for the Lord, would fulfill only one of those tasks? Of course not! We can be sure he fulfilled the total mission the Lord had given him.

We have proof later when the apostle Paul himself testified of how he spoke in tongues:

I thank my God, I speak with tongues more than ye all.

1 Corinthians 14:18

I have given you five scriptural references describing the baptism in the Holy Spirit and the sign of speaking in tongues. Even if someone tries to argue with the last two events, it is difficult to argue with the first three. So as Jesus said:

...that in the mouth of two or three witnesses every word may be established.

Matthew 18:16

These five examples are for a witness to the fact that speaking in tongues is the sign of the baptism in the Holy Spirit.

- **Why would God choose tongues as the initial sign?**

The Lord doesn't specify why He chose tongues as the initial sign, but let me share a few reasons why He might use this sign.

First, *it is obviously supernatural*. The Bible says God confirms His Word with signs and wonders. (Mark 16:20; Acts 2:17-19.)

If God had made the sign of receiving the baptism of the Holy Spirit as merely a high voice, or a muscle twitch, or a skin rash, or some other physical manifestation, people would always be able to explain it away with normal reasoning.

But when you begin to supernaturally speak in an unknown language, you know it isn't some staged or coincidental event! Jesus said it best:

Then said Jesus unto him, Except ye see signs and wonders, ye will not believe.

John 4:48

Second, *it requires faith and submission*.

You must believe in the Lord and trust Him. If you don't have enough faith to surrender everything to Him (including your tongue), you will probably not receive. The Lord will not force you to receive, and He does not normally give to an unwilling participant.

Thirdly, *it shows the power of God.*

God often emphasized the power and importance of the tongue. The Scriptures say that the tongue is hard to control; that it is razor sharp, deadly; and that no man can tame it. What better member of the body to show God's power? Remember, nothing is impossible with God! (See James 3:5-9; Ps. 52:2; Prov. 18:21; Jer. 9:8.)

• How does speaking in tongues work?

Basically, you speak in tongues as the Holy Spirit gives you the utterance. In other words, as He tells you what to say, you say it.

All you have to do is open your mouth and speak — He gives you the language.

> **And they were all filled with the Holy Ghost, and began to speak with other tongues, as the Spirit gave them utterance.**
>
> **Acts 2:4**

> **Likewise the Spirit also helpeth our infirmities: for we know not what we should pray for as we ought: but the Spirit itself maketh intercession for us with groanings which cannot be uttered.**
>
> **Romans 8:26**

The key to the release of tongues is your having faith in God's promises. One of Jesus' promises is the baptism of the Holy Spirit. He said:

> **...ye shall be baptized with the Holy Ghost not many days hence.**
>
> **Acts 1:5**

• How can I know that an utterance I receive is really from God?

The Scriptures give us the answer to your question:

> Hereby know ye the Spirit of God: Every spirit that
> confesseth that Jesus Christ is come in the flesh is of
> God:
> And every spirit that confesseth not that Jesus
> Christ is come in the flesh is not of God....
>
> 1 John 4:2,3

If the message you hear does not follow the teachings of
Jesus, then it is not from the Holy Spirit. But if you continue
to seek the Holy Spirit and His promises, He will make you
aware of any such false messages.

- **Once I have prayed for the baptism in the Holy
  Spirit, how do I get "tongues"; how does it start?**

Like you have said, the first and most important step is to
pray and ask Jesus to baptize you in the Holy Spirit.

Many people make the mistake of just asking for tongues,
but speaking in tongues is a result of the baptism of the Holy
Spirit, not the other way around. So don't seek tongues; seek
Jesus and the Holy Spirit.

Usually, speaking in tongues is just a natural flow
accompanying the baptism. There is no thunder, lightning or
any great dramatics to signify the baptism of the Holy Spirit.
Simply ask in faith expecting to receive. Let God do the rest.

When you have been baptized in the Holy Spirit, He will
begin to give you these strange unfamiliar words; hence the
phrase *unknown tongue* (or language). All you have to do is
speak it out!

But make no mistake, *you* have to do the speaking. The
Holy Spirit will not force any words out of your mouth. If you
release yourself to Him, the words will come out of your
innermost being. That's where the Holy Spirit lives!

I know it seems impossible. The whole concept is mind
boggling — but, then again, it's God!

You will never run out of words when you are praising God
with the Holy Spirit's help.

An important thing to remember is that *you* will not speak
in tongues unless *you speak*!

Many people will actually receive the baptism in the Holy Spirit, and even hear the words in their mind, but just not speak them forth.

Some are too stubborn, some still doubt the authenticity of it, some are even afraid to speak those words.

Unfortunately, these individuals go away incomplete, but they can still share their testimonies with others.

Satan will use such things to confuse both unbelievers and those who are seeking the baptism; he wants them to continue doubting the reality of the Holy Spirit. When he throws in a little doubt, he will cause many to simply abandon their search.

There is, without a doubt, a step of faith required in order to speak in tongues.

- **If it is so easy, why have I not yet spoken in tongues?**

For many, it is because they are not knowledgeable about Holy Spirit baptism or, more specifically, because they haven't tried!

If you are a born-again believer, you must first ask Jesus to baptize you in the Holy Spirit. Then there is no reason why you cannot speak in tongues.

The experience can be somewhat related to a child learning to speak. A newborn baby immediately has the ability to speak. He has vocal cords, lung capacity and lips to form words. So the physical means are in place. It is the mental part that has not yet made the connection; he does not know how to form words. After prompting from his parents, he reaches a certain point when he realizes he can speak and then desires to speak. He begins speaking phrases until he has a fluent language. Before long, speaking becomes second nature.

It is a similar experience with speaking in tongues. Once you are born into the family of Christ through salvation, you immediately have the prerequisite for speaking in tongues: the infilling of the Holy Spirit, which comes with salvation.

Then, at some point, you learn that there is moı
Holy Spirit, so you ask for the baptism. This mental de   ...ıs
the gate to receiving Holy Spirit baptism and speaking in
tongues. Like with that child, this new language simply
becomes second nature.

**And all things, whatsoever ye shall ask in prayer,
believing, ye shall receive.**

Matthew 21:22

• **To be honest, "tongues" seems impossible.**

Sure, it seems impossible, because we are always viewing
things with human, not heavenly, eyes. Anything supernatural
seems impossible because it is just what it says: *super-natural*
— more than natural, above the natural.

But as Christians we know that anything is possible
through God. Jesus told us!

**And Jesus looking upon them saith, With men it is
impossible, but not with God: for with God all things
are possible.**

Mark 10:27

(See also Matt. 19:26; Luke 18:27.)

When dealing with the things of God, we often have to
overcome our limited, logical thinking. I'm not saying you
should get illogical; I'm only saying that God sometimes
supernaturally exceeds logic.

Remember the following when you are trying to accept
tongues or any other supernatural thing from God:

1. Godly/spiritual/heavenly things do not always make sense
to us in the natural.

2. God's Word is Truth, regardless of whether we completely
understand it!

3. We are called to obey God's Word.

4. We must reach a point in which we step out in faith and
allow God to transcend our own understanding.

71

- **To me, "tongues" sounds like nonsense, just gibberish!**

In our human minds it sometimes does, so you are correct. But remember, tongues is an *unknown* language.

A language that comes to mind is that of the Bushmen of Africa and Australia. Their language includes many clicks and clucks of the tongue that sound like nonsense to the outsider. That, however, makes them no less of a language.

Also, don't forget that the Bible says we speak with the languages of men and of angels:

> **Though I speak with the tongues of men and of angels....**
>
> **1 Corinthians 13:1**

You might recognize a language of man, but what does an angel sound like? Probably gibberish to you and me!

What it boils down to is that the supernatural is often difficult to comprehend, and people will try to dismiss it as nonsense.

This is what nonbelievers try to do with God and Jesus. But that in no way lessens Their reality!

- **Is tongues always in an "unknown" language?**

Tongues is always an unknown language to the *speaker* but not always to the *hearer*.

There have been many cases in which one person was speaking in tongues and another person recognized it as his natural language. In every case the hearer confirmed that the speaker either had a message for the hearer, was praying to God, or was praising God.

In such cases the Lord chooses to supernaturally reveal Himself to an individual to get his attention. The hearer always reports that his language was spoken perfectly, in the most beautiful, flowing, proper form. In other words, it was presented in a way to insure the hearer that it was no coincidence and not something merely learned from a book.

The Bible records the instance at Pentecost when the disciples and all those in the upper room were speaking in many known languages:

> **And they were all filled with the Holy Ghost, and began to speak with other tongues, as the Spirit gave them utterance.**
>
> **And there were dwelling at Jerusalem Jews, devout men, out of every nation under heaven.**
>
> **Now when this was noised abroad, the multitude came together, and were confounded, because that every man heard them speak in his own language.**
>
> **And they were all amazed and marvelled, saying one to another, Behold, are not all these which speak Galilaeans?**
>
> **And how hear we every man in our own tongue, wherein we were born?**
>
> **Parthians, and Medes, and Elamites, and the dwellers in Mesopotamia, and in Judaea, and Cappadocia, in Pontus, and Asia,**
>
> **Phrygia, and Pamphylia, in Egypt, and in the parts of Libya about Cyrene, and strangers of Rome, Jews and proselytes,**
>
> **Cretes and Arabians, we do hear them speak in our tongues the wonderful works of God.**
>
> Acts 2:4-11

Notice this says there were men from many nations, and many different "known" languages were heard. Also the speakers were recognized as Galileans; in other words, they had no natural knowledge of the languages they spoke. Then the Scriptures record the subject of their tongues as **the wonderful works of God** (v. 11).

- **When you pray in tongues, does it always sound the same?**

Not always; but most of the time it will sound basically the same.

From time to time, however, you will find that when you speak in tongues the sound may vary. There is often a difference, depending on your reason for praying. Praise, prayer and thanksgiving may take on different sounds as you speak in tongues with these topics in mind.

For example, when I am praying for my own needs, the language may sound distinctly different from when I am praying for others. When I pray in tongues for someone to receive a physical healing, the tongues can sound different from when I am praying for the healing of a relationship.

But doesn't that make sense? The Holy Spirit prays a different kind of prayer for each individual need.

> **Likewise the Spirit also helpeth our infirmities: for we know not what we should pray for as we ought: but the Spirit itself maketh intercession for us with groanings which cannot be uttered.**
>
> **Romans 8:26**

Occasionally, while in prayer, the tongues I normally speak will change into a deep, pleading type of tongues. It's difficult to explain, but I would liken it to someone praying to save a child's life. It is that kind of heart-wrenching, emotional prayer. We are children of God, and the Holy Spirit is indeed pleading for the needs in our lives.

Now don't be concerned if your spiritual language does not sound like that of other people. Everyone's language sounds a little different, and some are drastically different. There are no patterns for tongues. The Holy Spirit gives each person his own individual language.

Your spiritual language may be short and choppy or smooth and fluent. It may be slow and methodic or fast and furious. It matters not!

What matters is that you are obedient to allow the Holy Spirit to flow through you.

- **When I speak in tongues, will I know what I'm saying?**

  Let me answer this in parts.

First, generally when you speak in tongues, you don't understand word for word what you are saying. You simply speak forth the words as the Holy Spirit prompts you. Like the apostle Paul wrote to the Corinthians:

> **For if I pray in a tongue, my spirit prays, but my mind is unfruitful. So what shall I do? I will pray with my spirit, but I will also pray with my mind....**
> **1 Corinthians 14:14,15 (NIV)**

In other words, when you speak in tongues, your mind does not determine the next word you will say. The Holy Spirit gives you the words. Conversely, your choice of words in your normal everyday language is always controlled by your mind.

Supernaturally, you will know in your mind and heart that the Holy Spirit is addressing the specific prayer request you have brought to His attention. You will sense it, and you will know in your spirit the subject of your prayer.

In the same manner, you will discern when the prayer has been completed. Although you may not understand the specific words you are praying, you will know the reason for your prayers.

- **Where can I speak in tongues? only in church?**

No, it works anywhere! Remember, the Holy Spirit is in you; He goes where you go. So any manifestation of the Spirit is available wherever you are.

The Holy Spirit is a great Comforter; He is the Light in your closet. Even when you shut the door, He is still turned on! He remains ready to brighten your world at all times. When you open the door, He will be there! He's the Light of your life that never goes out!

- **If I start speaking in tongues, will I lose control; can I stop and start again?**

Will you lose control? Absolutely not!

The Holy Spirit is a Gentleman. He will not cause you to do anything or act in any way that is against your nature.

Remember, *you* speak as the Holy Spirit gives *you* the utterance. That means He is giving you the words, but you do the speaking.

Can you stop and start at will? Absolutely! You have total control of speaking in tongues, and you are free to use your prayer language as often as you like. You can start anytime, anywhere, and you can stop just as quickly.

- **Will the Holy Spirit make me speak out in a crowd or cause me to do weird things?**

Goodness no! This is *God's* Spirit. He does not do crazy things or expect His children to do crazy things! He is the Comforter. (John 14:16,26.)

The Bible gives direction in the things of the Spirit:

Let all things be done decently and in order.
1 Corinthians 14:40

- **Why do you emphasize speaking in tongues?**

Speaking in tongues is obviously biblical. It was even a part of the disciples' lives. And, more importantly, the Bible says we should not forbid it:

Wherefore, brethren, covet to prophesy, and *forbid not to speak with tongues.*
1 Corinthians 14:39

I do not emphasize speaking in tongues as a solitary experience. Instead, I emphasize the baptism in the Holy Spirit. This is a promise of Jesus that is available to all who seek it.

Many wonderful things will happen in your life after you receive the baptism. Speaking in tongues is simply the *sign* of the baptism.

But the primary emphasis should always be the experience of receiving Jesus as personal Savior.

Jesus saith unto him, I am the way, the truth, and the life: no man cometh unto the Father, but by me.

John 14:6

The baptism of the Holy Spirit should always be secondary to salvation. However, that does not give us the right to dismiss the baptism as unimportant. It is very important to Jesus — He is the Baptizer!

- **Can I receive the baptism of the Holy Spirit and just leave off speaking in tongues?**

Based on the Scriptures and my personal experience, I believe that when you receive the baptism of the Holy Spirit, you will also receive the accompanying sign of tongues.

Let's look at some biblical accounts of Holy Spirit baptism. You will see that speaking in tongues is clearly a sign of the baptism.

The Day of Pentecost

And they were *all* filled with the Holy Ghost, and began to speak with other tongues, as the Spirit gave them utterance.

Acts 2:4

Peter and the House of Cornelius

While Peter yet spake these words, the Holy Ghost fell on *all* them which heard the word.

And they of the circumcision which believed were astonished, as many as came with Peter, because that on the Gentiles also was poured out the gift of the Holy Ghost.

For they heard them speak with tongues, and magnify God....

Acts 10:44-46

77

Paul and the Believers at Ephesus

And when Paul had laid his hands upon them, the Holy Ghost came on them; and they spake with tongues, and prophesied.
And *all* the men were about twelve.

Acts 19:6,7

Without question, the above Scriptures clearly indicate that speaking in tongues accompanies the baptism in the Holy Spirit. Also note that they *all* spoke in tongues.

Whether or not you believe that tongues always accompanies the baptism, you must agree that there is biblical precedence for speaking in tongues as the sign.

Now pay close attention to this: I am not saying you cannot receive the baptism in the Holy Spirit without *speaking* in tongues; I am saying you will not receive the baptism without *receiving* the tongues. In other words, you will always receive the tongues, but you may not speak forth the words. It is your choice.

During my ministry I have occasionally met people who feel they have received the baptism but have never spoken in tongues.

Over the years there have been many well-known pastors and evangelists who exhibited the power of the Holy Spirit but did not publicly profess to speaking in tongues.

Remember this: just because these people did not *speak* in tongues does not mean they were not *given* the tongues.

When Jesus baptizes someone in the Holy Spirit, the biblical pattern is for that person to receive a supernatural language of tongues.

If He gives *one* person an unknown tongue, then He will give *every* person an unknown tongue.

However, the Holy Spirit will not force us to move our mouths and speak out the words. It is our job to show submission and speak forth in faith.

God does not give tongues to some while refusing others. We have shown through the Scriptures that speaking in tongues is the sign of the baptism. Often, a person wants the baptism and is willing to ask for it but is fearful or reluctant to speak in tongues. Whenever we come to Jesus seeking the baptism, He will be faithful to do His part. Unfortunately, we are sometimes sluggish in doing our part.

If you truly seek the baptism in the Holy Spirit, Jesus will be faithful to you. He will give you your spiritual language of tongues, but it remains for you to speak it out.

This is where many people get stubborn. They are willing to *accept* this gift from the Lord, but they are not willing to *give* anything in return. He freely gives us this gift; all He asks is that we open our mouths and use it! God is not *changing the rules*; we are trying to *rule the change*.

Also, the Bible says, ...**forbid not to speak in tongues** (1 Cor. 14:39). I would not want to be in the position where I know God's will but then directly oppose it!·

My friend, the baptism in the Holy Spirit and tongues is a package deal. If you seek one, you should expect the other. As I heard someone say long ago, "When you buy a new pair of shoes, the tongue comes with it!"

- **I've heard that people who aren't even saved have spoken in tongues. Is this possible?**

This is not scriptural and is directly against the principles of the Bible.

Two possibilities exist: either the person who told you this was mistaken about that other person's salvation, or if such an event occurred it was a counterfeit of the devil.

You cannot speak in tongues under God's power unless you have received Jesus as your Lord and Savior *and* have received the baptism of the Holy Spirit.

•Do I "have" to speak in tongues?

No, you don't *have* to — you *get* to!

Nothing in the Scriptures says you *have* to speak in tongues. In fact, there's nothing in the Scriptures that says you *have* to do anything! It says only that in order for you to get good things certain other things must be accomplished. You don't have to believe in Jesus at all, but to be saved you certainly do!

God does not force us into anything. Instead, He gives us a choice. He shows us the choice He wants us to make, but the decision is still ours.

He wants us to choose to receive the baptism in the Holy Spirit. Why else would He have sent the Holy Spirit to be our Comforter? Why else would He show us the wonderful things the disciples and early believers received due to the Holy Spirit?

It would be like winning a million dollars, then saying, "Do I *have* to take it?" Of course not, but once you realize its value, you will desire it!

You should earnestly seek *all* of God's promises, including speaking in tongues!

• **Why should I speak in tongues?**

The answer is simple: because it is a special way to communicate with God. First Corinthians 14:2 says:

> **He that speaketh in an unknown tongue speaketh not unto men, but unto God....**

There are many reasons why it is God's will that we speak in tongues; so many, in fact, that it is difficult to know where to start. But to help you understand, I have included ten reasons below.

Speaking in tongues is the sign of the baptism in the Holy Spirit.

As we have discussed, the sign showing that you have received the baptism in the Holy Spirit is speaking in tongues. Read again the following Scriptures:

Pentecost   Acts 2:4
Peter at the house of Cornelius   Acts 10:46
Paul and the Ephesians   Acts 19:6

Speaking in tongues
edifies you spiritually.

Edify means to build up.[2] Speaking in tongues builds you up when you're down; it encourages and comforts you.

> **He that speaketh in an unknown tongue edifieth himself; but he that prophesieth edifieth the church.**
> **1 Corinthians 14:4**

Speaking in tongues will help you
in your prayer life!

A. Speaking in tongues allows you to speak directly to God!

> **For he that speaketh in an unknown tongue speaketh not unto men, but unto God: for no man understandeth him; howbeit in the spirit he speaketh mysteries.**
> **1 Corinthians 14:2**

B. Speaking in tongues balances your prayer life.

> **...I will pray with the spirit, and I will pray with the understanding also: I will sing with the spirit, and I will sing with the understanding also.**
> **1 Corinthians 14:15**

Speaking in tongues allows
the Holy Spirit to intercede for us!

The Holy Spirit will intercede and express things which you cannot within the boundaries of your natural language.

> Likewise the Spirit also helpeth our infirmities: for
> we know not what we should pray for as we ought....
> **Romans 8:26**

Speaking in tongues allows us to pray for the "unknown"
and ensures that we remain in the will of God.

> ...but the Spirit itself maketh intercession for us
> with groanings which cannot be uttered.
>
> And he that searcheth the hearts knoweth what is
> the mind of the Spirit, because he maketh intercession
> for the saints according to the will of God.
> **Romans 8:26,27**

Speaking in tongues helps us to praise and worship the Lord.

> ...I will pray with the spirit, and I will pray with
> the understanding also: I will sing with the spirit, and
> I will sing with the understanding also.
> **1 Corinthians 14:15**

Speaking in tongues is a sign to the unbeliever.

> Wherefore tongues are for a sign, not to them that
> believe, but to them that believe not....
> **1 Corinthians 14:22**

Speaking in tongues is a constant reminder of the Holy Spirit's presence within you!

The gift of tongues comes from the Holy Spirit, and the
Holy Spirit lives in you. (1 Cor. 12:10; 3:16.) Therefore, when
you speak in tongues, it is a supernatural reminder of the
presence of God's Spirit within you.

The Spirit itself beareth witness with our spirit, that we are the children of God.

Romans 8:16

Speaking in tongues is a sign of confirmation to the crucifixion, resurrection and promises of Jesus Christ!

- We know Jesus was crucified, buried and resurrected.
- We know after being resurrected Jesus appeared to the disciples and many others, and was finally taken up to heaven. (Acts 1:8-11; Mark 16:19; Luke 24:51.)
- We know Jesus said this:

Nevertheless I tell you the truth; It is expedient for you that I go away: for if I go not away, the Comforter will not come unto you; but if I depart, I will send him unto you.

John 16:7

- We know "the Comforter" is the Holy Spirit. (John 14:26.)
- We know the Holy Spirit gives spiritual gifts, including the gift of tongues. (1 Cor. 12:8-11.)
- It all adds up! When we speak in tongues, we are testifying and witnessing that Jesus is true to His promises.

Speaking in tongues shows submission to the Holy Spirit and to Jesus.

Jesus is the Baptizer, and the Holy Spirit gives the gift of tongues; so when you pray in tongues, you show your submission and obedience to Them.

Praying always with all prayer and supplication in the Spirit, and watching thereunto with all perseverance and supplication for all saints;
And for me, that utterance may be given unto me, that I may open my mouth boldly, to make known the mystery of the gospel.

Ephesians 6:18,19

God said so!

Wherefore, brethren, covet to prophesy, and forbid not to speak with tongues.

1 Corinthians 14:39

But ye, beloved, building up yourselves on your most holy faith, praying in the Holy Ghost.

Jude 20

Speaking in tongues in your private devotions will lead you into a new level of spiritual maturity. The Holy Spirit will lead you, guide you and teach you many truths as you allow Him to flow through you.

For myself and so many others, speaking in tongues has enhanced our prayer life in measures that cannot be described.

The baptism of the Holy Spirit will open new doors into greater spiritual insight as He reveals the Scriptures to you.

* **Do you believe that only those who speak in tongues will get to heaven?**

Of course not! There is no biblical basis for this belief. In fact, anyone telling you this has been deceived.

True, you will definitely be helped in your spiritual walk because the Holy Spirit opens the Word to you and gives you an excitement. But it is by no means a prerequisite to salvation.

The Scriptures make it very plain. Jesus said:

He that believeth and is baptized shall be saved; but he that believeth not shall be damned.

Mark 16:16

I am the door: by me if any man enter in, he shall be saved....

John 10:9

There is obviously no emphasis on speaking in tongues as being necessary to enter the kingdom of God. The only requirement God gave us was to accept Jesus as the Savior.

The baptism of the Holy Spirit and speaking in tongues will never save you. That's not its purpose. However, it can lead you into a new and exciting relationship with Christ, which will keep you walking the narrow path.

- **What about tongues being "of the devil"?**

Would you believe me if I told you that this statement itself is from the devil? Even Jesus Himself had to deal with this old trick!

> **And the scribes which came down from Jerusalem said, He hath Beelzebub, and by the prince of the devils casteth he out devils.**
>
> **Mark 3:22**

This is great for Satan because it fulfills a twofold function. First, it hinders and confuses people so they will not learn more about the Holy Spirit and God's Word. Second, it gives him credit for this supernatural gift from God. And he will grab the glory whenever he can!

But let's look at the facts. Jesus, in speaking of believers, said in Mark 16:17, ...**they shall speak with new tongues.** Let me repeat: *Jesus said it!* Does that sound like it's from the devil?

• • •

Let me give you three pieces of advice:

1. It is true that the devil will try to counterfeit the Holy Spirit (as he does all of God's works).
2. Everything you encounter should be checked against God's Word to make sure it is in line with God. I have shown you many, many Scriptures in this book confirming that speaking in tongues is of God.
3. If you ask to receive the Holy Spirit from Jesus, you need not fear experiencing something from the devil. Jesus is much more powerful than the devil!

• • •

God's Word says:

> **Submit yourselves therefore to God. Resist the devil, and he will flee from you.**
>
> **James 4:7**

The Word also says that the Lord will not try to trick you, and He will not allow Satan to substitute anything other than what you ask for from the Lord. As Jesus said:

> **If a son shall ask bread of any of you that is a father, will he give him a stone? or if he ask a fish, will he for a fish give him a serpent?**
>
> **Or if he shall ask an egg, will he offer him a scorpion?**
>
> **If ye then, being evil, know how to give good gifts unto your children: how much more shall your heavenly Father give the Holy Spirit to them that ask him?**
>
> **Luke 11:11-13**

Speaking in tongues is scriptural; it is truth. When the words come out of Jesus Himself regarding the Holy Spirit, it's time to keep quiet about the devil.

- **If Jesus is our Example, why is there no record of Him speaking in tongues?**

First, let's make sure we all understand the terminology. There should be a distinction between *speaking in tongues* and the *baptism in the Holy Spirit.*

It is important that people come to the realization that these two experiences are not equal! One is a subset of the other. The baptism in the Holy Spirit is the life-changing event; speaking in tongues is the sign that it has happened.

Because speaking in tongues is the most "advertised" gift, people tend to lift it to a higher position. But this is still only a part of the real gift of God, which is the baptism in the Holy Spirit.

True, Jesus had the power of the Holy Spirit dwelling within Him, but at that time *only* Jesus had that power. The Holy Spirit had not yet been sent to live within the believers. Tongues was a gift of the Holy Spirit (the Comforter), and He was not with us until after Jesus had left the earth. Jesus said:

Nevertheless I tell you the truth; It is expedient for you that I go away: for if I go not away, the Comforter will not come unto you; but if I depart, I will send him unto you.

John 16:7

And these signs shall follow them that believe; In my name shall they cast out devils; they shall speak with new tongues.

Mark 16:17

The need for this *sign* did not exist before the day of Pentecost. After that initial outpouring of the Holy Spirit, the sign of speaking in tongues followed everyone who received the baptism. The day of Pentecost ushered in the era of the Holy Spirit in which we now live.

Speaking in tongues is the sign of the baptism in the Holy Spirit — the same Holy Spirit Who was sent to the earth *after* Jesus had left. When Jesus was here, people could see Him in the flesh. Just as He had a sign like a dove when He was baptized at the River Jordan, another sign — tongues — was created after He was gone, so that the unbelievers would recognize the baptism of the Holy Spirit.

- **But doesn't the Bible say, "tongues will cease"?**

This phrase is found in the famous "Love Chapter," chapter 13 of First Corinthians. The whole context of this chapter is explaining the tremendous importance of love (or charity) in everything we do.

In the following Scripture, the apostle Paul is making the point that all of the things which deal with mankind will eventually disappear when we are with the Father. He is saying that love (or charity) which comes from the Father, will be with us always.

> **Charity** (love) **never faileth: but whether there be prophecies, they shall fail; whether there be tongues, they shall cease; whether there be knowledge, it shall vanish away.**
>
> 1 Corinthians 13:8

The purpose of this Scripture is not to indicate that tongues have somehow gone away. There is no basis for this idea. We can't take one Scripture verse and use it out of context with the rest of the Bible.

Has *knowledge* gone away? No! And nobody would argue that. But the Scripture treats knowledge the same as tongues. This Scripture has been used as a feeble attempt to suggest that tongues is not for today. With regard to people who are teaching this untruth, I sometimes wonder if perhaps knowledge did indeed go away — from them!

The real reason behind this Scripture is that there will be no purpose for any of these earthly items once we get to heaven. We will be all-knowing, we will know all languages, there will be no reason to prophesy — we will be with God! All of these needs will already have been met.

Some try to argue against tongues based on the following Scripture:

> **But when that which is perfect is come, then that which is in part shall be done away.**
>
> 1 Corinthians 13:10

This argument centers around the belief that the word **perfect** in this Scripture refers to the New Testament, and that once the New Testament is complete, there will be no use for tongues.

My response is threefold. First, there is no support for this argument anywhere else in the Scriptures. Secondly, it is widely accepted that **perfect** here refers to the second coming of Christ. Thirdly, even if it did refer to the New Testament, how does the phrase **that which is in part** apply only to tongues? Frankly, it doesn't.

Since speaking in tongues is a gift of the Holy Spirit, the following sums it up quite well:

> ...**for God's gifts and his call are irrevocable.**
>
> **Romans 11:29** (NIV)

His gifts will not leave us until we leave this earth! *thank you*

The bottom line is that although the apostle Paul gave many instructions regarding tongues and interpretation, he never once said, "Do not speak in tongues!" He merely gave instructions on how to keep church services orderly. But the orderly church service he described still included speaking in tongues. In fact, Paul encouraged speaking in tongues:

> **I would that ye all spake with tongues....**
>
> **1 Corinthians 14:5**

- **What about those who say that speaking in tongues is "emotionalism"?**

This often disturbs those who are satisfied with a more dignified or conservative form of worship. Let me answer your question in two ways.

First, speaking in tongues is totally under the control of the individual. Therefore, he may choose when and where to speak in tongues. He will never suddenly burst loose with tongues in some explosion of emotion. The speaker has control. He can also pray silently to himself if the situation is not conducive to free worship.

Second, who started the rumor that it is bad to show emotions in church? It certainly wasn't God! Numerous Scriptures throughout the Bible tell us to praise God with everything we have!

God created us as humans with a wide range of emotions, such as joy, sadness, remorse and elation. We cannot ignore the fact that we possess these emotions. They are God given.

When we enter into the presence of God, we will often experience one or more of these emotions. At such times it is not atypical, for example, to see a man cry. It is a beautiful thing when he has been touched by God.

Unfortunately over the years, men have developed this concept of the grave, immovable, silent congregation that should simply listen and not respond. I sometimes call them the "Chosen Frozen"!

Remember, my friend, these things are from man, not God! God wants you to respond to Him. Would you like to have a conversation with someone who never acknowledges that he is listening and receiving what you have to say? I don't think so.

During a football game people can get really worked up, so excited that they clap, laugh and shout for joy, showing unhindered their true feelings of happiness.

But those same people have placed God in a box and have put us in there with Him. We can talk about God only in church, and then only in the most quiet, reverent way.

Why is excitement over God labeled as "fanaticism"? Why shouldn't we show as much joy for our God as we do for our sports heroes? Things are definitely out of balance, and we need to restore that feeling of excitement about God!

Even when the apostle Paul wrote to the Corinthians, he did not rebuke them for the tongues, prophecy and other gifts of God; he simply put them in order. He never spoke against any of the gifts they were displaying but rather against their methods. In the same manner, things like speaking in tongues and showing joy are not to be dismissed, but only controlled.

Now you may be saying that this proves your point about emotionalism not belonging in church. However, the cure for abuse is not to *remove* that person, but to *correct* that person. The apostle Paul did not kick any of those Corinthians out of church membership!

Also, Paul did not tell those church members to only sit and listen to the minister. He allowed them to continue an active part in the worship service. He allowed them to speak out in the service if they had a word from God. He merely told them to do it in an orderly fashion.

The manner in which a person acts and reacts in his worship is due very much to the person and the setting. A normally energetic individual may seem reserved when in a more reserved type of service. But that same person may seem loud when the service allows prayers and emotions to be expressed more freely during praise and worship.

Please don't let the actions of others, or the rumors you have heard, keep you from the Truth that is shown in God's Word.

- **Why do some people call tongues an "ecstatic utterance"?**

The truth? Because those people are ignorant of the reality of tongues!

Though this phrase is occasionally used to describe tongues, it is in no way biblically based. The Scriptures use the word *utterance* but never *ecstatic*. This implies that tongues is a wild, emotional chattering that has no meaning, but the Bible simply calls it *speaking* in tongues. There is no indication of any uncontrollable chatter.

The idea that a person who is speaking in tongues goes off into some type of uncontrollable "mumbo jumbo" is not supported, either biblically or with experience.

- **Doesn't the Bible insinuate in the book of First Corinthians that everyone does not speak in tongues?**

This is a common misunderstanding. But the answer is really very clear if we examine the Scriptures. First, let's review the Scripture to which you referred:

> **And God hath set some in the church, first apostles, secondarily prophets, thirdly teachers, after that miracles, then gifts of healings, helps, governments, diversities of tongues.**
> **Are all apostles? are all prophets? are all teachers? are all workers of miracles?**

> **Have all the gifts of healing? do all speak with tongues? do all interpret?**
>
> **1 Corinthians 12:28-30**

The obvious answer to this question is, *No!* So, many Christians use this Scripture as an argument that they should not speak in tongues.

But we can't just stop there.

From the context of the Scripture, it is obvious that we are discussing *gifts* to the Church, both the ministry gifts and the spiritual gifts. So, it follows that this Scripture relates to the gift of divers tongues.

As additional proof, the Scripture references the gifts of working of miracles, healings and interpretation of tongues. This latter gift is always associated with the gift of divers tongues. True, all do not receive the gift of divers tongues because, *like all of the gifts*, the Holy Spirit determines the distribution of the gifts.

But what about speaking in tongues as the sign of the baptism of the Holy Spirit? As we examine the following Scriptures, notice that *everyone* who received the baptism spoke in tongues:

The Day of Pentecost

> **And they were all filled with the Holy Ghost, and began to speak with other tongues, as the Spirit gave them utterance.**
>
> **Acts 2:4**

Peter and the House of Cornelius

> **While Peter yet spake these words, the Holy Ghost fell on all them which heard the word.**
>
> **For they heard them speak with tongues, and magnify God.**
>
> **Acts 10:44,46**

Paul and the Believers at Ephesus

And when Paul had laid his hands upon them, the Holy Ghost came on them; and they spake with tongues, and prophesied.

And all the men were about twelve.

Acts 19:6,7

Saul (Paul) and Ananias

And Ananias went his way, and entered into the house; and putting his hands on him said, Brother Saul (Paul), the Lord, even Jesus, that appeared unto thee in the way as thou camest, hath sent me, that thou mightest receive thy sight, and be filled with the Holy Ghost.

Acts 9:17

Paul (Saul) Confirms his Baptism with the Holy Ghost

I thank my God, I speak with tongues more than ye all.

1 Corinthians 14:18

It is evident in the above Scriptures that in every case where they received the baptism of the Holy Spirit, they *all* spoke in tongues. Since God does not change, this is still the sign of the baptism of the Holy Spirit. And *everyone* should expect to speak in tongues.

It is also obvious that the above Scriptures do *not* refer to the *gift* of divers tongues. The prayer language that you receive with the baptism of the Holy Spirit is separate from the *gift* of divers tongues. The *gifts* are distributed as the Holy Spirit chooses, but the *sign* — speaking in tongues — remains the same for everyone.

"2" Kinds tongues

[1]James H. Strong, *Strong's Exhaustive Concordance*, Compact ed. (Grand Rapids: Baker, Reprinted 1992), "Greek Dictionary of the New Testament," p. 20, #1100.

[2]James H. Strong, *Strong's Exhaustive Concordance*, Compact ed. (Grand Rapids: Baker, Reprinted 1992), "Greek Dictionary of the New Testament," p. 51, #3618.

4

How To Receive
the Baptism of the Holy Spirit

Now that we know Who the Holy Spirit is and what Holy Spirit baptism is, the next obvious question is, "How do I receive?"

This chapter focuses on methods for receiving and administering the baptism of the Holy Spirit.

- **What is the sequence of events leading to the baptism in the Holy Spirit?**

There are several distinct "events" which may lead to the baptism, but there is only one prerequisite: the acceptance of Jesus Christ as your Lord and Savior. That is the *only* step which *must* be taken before you can receive the baptism in the Holy Spirit.

Here is a typical scenario:

1. An individual hears the Word of God.
2. He believes the Word.
3. He accepts Christ as his Savior.
4. He follows in water baptism.
5. He prays and asks for the baptism in the Holy Spirit.
6. He receives the baptism in the Holy Spirit.

Again, this is the most typical sequence of events but not the only possibility.

The first three steps always occur in this order; the last three may vary in sequence. A person could receive the baptism in the Holy Spirit either *before*, *after* or *during* water baptism. The only requirement is that he must already have accepted Jesus as Savior. Some individuals may receive the baptism in the Holy Spirit immediately, almost simultaneously, after receiving Jesus as Savior.

But make no mistake about it, the baptism in the Holy Spirit is a definite, distinct, separate event in a believer's life. A person should never just *assume* he has received the baptism in the Holy Spirit. When he has received, he will *know* it!

- **How do you get baptized in the Holy Spirit? Must a minister always be involved?**

Before we discuss the methods for receiving the baptism, let's talk about prerequisites. There is only one prerequisite, but then two steps:

1. *You must be saved*, having accepted Jesus Christ as your Lord and Savior.
2. Then, *you believe and receive.*

It is possible to receive Holy Spirit baptism upon salvation without specifically asking for it, but that is not the norm. It has been my experience that a person will not receive the baptism unless he is truly seeking the Lord for it.

Here is the way it works: Jesus is the Baptizer. (Surprised? You shouldn't be.) He is the only One in all the Bible to Whom that duty is given. John the Baptist says plainly in the Scriptures:

> **And I knew him not: but he that sent me to baptize with water, the same said unto me, Upon whom thou shalt see the Spirit descending, and remaining on him, the same is he which baptizeth with the Holy Ghost.**
>
> **John 1:33**

(See also Matt. 3:11; Mark 1:8; Luke 3:16.)

Now if that isn't proof enough, Jesus Himself testifies to the Truth:

> **And, being assembled together with them, (Jesus) commanded them that they should not depart from**

Jerusalem, but wait for the promise of the Father, which, saith he, ye have heard of me.

For John truly baptized with water; but ye shall be baptized with the Holy Ghost not many days hence.

Acts 1:4,5

Later the apostle Peter testifies to what Jesus had said:

Then remembered I the word of the Lord, how that he said, John indeed baptized with water; but ye shall be baptized with the Holy Ghost.

Acts 11:16

The apostle Paul speaks of the Holy Spirit being poured out *through* Jesus:

Not by works of righteousness which we have done, but according to his mercy he saved us, by the washing of regeneration, and renewing of the Holy Ghost;

Which he shed on us abundantly through Jesus Christ our Saviour.

Titus 3:5,6

Now that you know Jesus is the Baptizer, what is the most important thing you should do? Accept Jesus as your Lord and Savior. You cannot truly believe in this baptism if you do not believe in the Baptizer!

This is really all that is required for you to receive the baptism. You can receive it in your own home with no one else around or at church with thousands around. It's truly between you and Jesus.

But there is nothing wrong with asking someone to assist you in receiving. Many, many people (including myself) have received the baptism through the help of other Christians. It might be your pastor or an elder in your church, but it can be any person who believes in Christ and has the faith to help.

These "helpers" will not actually give you the baptism; that power still remains with Jesus. Their purpose is to join their faith together with yours. Then Jesus will work *through* them to administer the baptism to you.

- **Can you show me how to receive the baptism of the Holy Spirit?**

  Once a person is receptive to the idea of Holy Spirit baptism, the next question he asks is, "How do I receive the Holy Spirit?"

  The hardest concept to grasp is that the baptism is a *supernatural* event. There really is no set formula you can follow to automatically receive this experience. As with many spiritual truths, the Lord wants your faith to function. He can choose any way, any time and any place to pour out His Spirit upon you.

  This is a difficult concept for some people to accept. They want a detailed, step-by-step process to follow, or they want God to just zap them!

  The Lord did not spell it out in a list, but He also did not leave us without a clue. As always, He uses the Bible to show us how to apply His Word. In the same manner, He gives us several specific examples to show the various ways in which the baptism can be received.

  If you feel you need some step-by-step instructions in order to receive, I have provided some suggestions. These are scripturally based guidelines that will prepare you and help you to understand.

Accept Jesus
as your Lord and Savior.

This is the first and only requirement. Without it, nothing else will happen.

> **Jesus saith unto him, I am the way, the truth, and the life: no man cometh unto the Father, but by me.**
> **John 14:6**

> **That if thou shalt confess with thy mouth the Lord Jesus, and shalt believe in thine heart that God hath raised him from the dead, thou shalt be saved.**
> **Romans 10:9**

You can only accept Jesus as the Son of God if you have already received the God Who sent Him. In the same manner, for you to receive the Holy Spirit you must first receive the One Who sent Him — Jesus!

Understand that you "already" have the Holy Spirit inside you.

The Holy Spirit is a Gift from God. He was given to you when you were saved, and He is dwelling inside you! All that's required now is the release that the baptism brings.

And we have seen and do testify that the Father sent the Son to be the Saviour of the world.

Whosoever shall confess that Jesus is the Son of God, God dwelleth in him, and he in God.

1 John 4:14,15

Understand that any Christian can receive Holy Spirit baptism.

There are no special requirements for receiving the Holy Spirit. You don't have to be "someone special," like a preacher or a Bible teacher.

Then Peter opened his mouth, and said, Of a truth I perceive that God is no respecter of persons.

Acts 10:34

The only requirement is that you be saved, having accepted Jesus Christ as your Lord and Savior. God makes things easy! He didn't want this to be difficult.

God gave the Holy Spirit for *everyone*:

For the promise is unto you, and to your children, and to all that are afar off, even as many as the Lord our God shall call.

Acts 2:39

Pray, then ask!

Prayer plays a very important part in the baptism of the Holy Spirit.

Let's look again at the portions of Scriptures pertaining to the baptism in the Holy Spirit, but this time I want you to notice that each group or individual was first involved in prayer.

Jesus

Now when all the people were baptized, it came to pass, that Jesus also being baptized, *and praying*, the heaven was opened,

And the Holy Ghost descended....

Luke 3:21,22

The 120 in the Upper Room

These all continued with one accord *in prayer* and supplication....

And they were all filled with the Holy Ghost, and began to speak with other tongues, as the Spirit gave them utterance.

Acts 1:14; 2:4

The Believers in the Early Church at Jerusalem

And when they heard that, they lifted up their voice to God with one accord....

And when they had *prayed*, the place was shaken where they were assembled together; and they were all filled with the Holy Ghost, and they spake the word of God with boldness.

Acts 4:24,31

Peter and John and the Samaritans

Now when the apostles which were at Jerusalem heard that Samaria had received the word of God, they sent unto them Peter and John:

Who, when they were come down, *prayed for them*, that they might receive the Holy Ghost.

Acts 8:14,15

Cornelius

And Cornelius said, Four days ago I was fasting until this hour; and at the ninth hour I *prayed* in my house....

Acts 10:30

Prayer opens up the doors of heaven to give you the promises of the Father. Do not forget the importance of praying as a part of seeking the baptism of the Holy Spirit, and receiving any other of God's promises as well.

Receive by faith.

The Holy Spirit is received by faith! Just like you had faith to receive Jesus, you must use faith to receive the baptism of the Holy Spirit.

It may be difficult at first to overcome the supernatural concept. It's not "logical," the way mankind thinks of things.

All God requires is for you to trust Him enough to take a step of faith, and He will be faithful to provide what you are asking. You are really saying, "I have faith that Jesus will fulfill His promises."

...the word preached did not profit them, not being mixed with faith in them that heard it.

Hebrews 4:2

Don't let "earthly logic" hinder "heavenly blessings"!

Set your mind to spiritual things rather than earthly things.

Remember, the Holy Spirit is from God and He is supernatural. Because the baptism is supernatural, it may seem unusual or illogical, but it does not change the truth that He is God!

The Holy Spirit is not a mysterious, frightening thing. He is a Friend. He is a part of the Trinity: God, Jesus, the Holy Spirit. He is as much love and grace as God Himself!

Don't worry about the devil!

God is more powerful than the devil! (Now read this statement again and really believe it!)

My friend, the devil will try as much as possible to deceive you. He will try to convince you that there's really no such thing as Holy Spirit baptism. But if that doesn't work, He will tell you, "That could never happen to you — you're not good enough!"

Do you know why Satan fights the baptism? Because it scares him!

He doesn't want you to receive the baptism because, through it, you will become stronger and more powerful in your Christian walk. He does not want a powerful enemy!

He will even tell you, "That baptism in the Holy Spirit is of the devil!" He loves to use that phrase *of the devil!* Not only does it scare people so that they will not receive, it also gives him credit for this miraculous gift from God!

Expect to speak in tongues.

This may sound strange, but it's important: the initial sign of the infilling of the Holy Spirit is speaking in tongues.

When you pray to receive the baptism of the Holy Spirit, you should *expect* to speak in tongues. That's proof that it has happened!

Some people have said they want the baptism but not tongues. That's not how it works, my friend.

The Holy Spirit and tongues is a package deal. Speaking in tongues is the initial evidence of receiving the baptism of the Holy Spirit.

If you are not ready to receive tongues, it may slow down your progress. If you're still scared, read the chapter on tongues again. There's nothing to be afraid of!

Submit yourself to God and be a willing vessel.

You have to *want* to receive. It's important that you seek God's Word and hunger for the baptism.

If you approach this with a wishy-washy attitude, you may never receive. But if you will approach it with an expectant, hopeful yearning, Jesus is *always* faithful to do His part.

It's okay to be a little nervous, maybe a little scared — that's natural — but don't let that hinder you from receiving.

Do your part!

You speak in tongues as the Holy Spirit gives *you* the words. The Holy Spirit does not speak in tongues, *you do*! He will give you the words, but you have to open your mouth and speak them.

Yes, it takes faith.

Yes, it's a little scary.

But remember you are dealing with God and Jesus. They love you and want the best for you. They will not embarrass or harm you. They are faithful to Their promises.

Just as Romans 10:9 says, you have to believe with your heart and confess with your mouth.

The apostle James wrote:

But be ye doers of the word, and not hearers only, deceiving your own selves.

James 1:22

Don't just stand there waiting for your spiritual language to come; open your mouth and begin to praise God. Once you have begun to speak, the Holy Spirit will simply give you new words to say. But if you keep your mouth closed, you may miss it!

• **If Jesus is the Baptizer, why do Scriptures call it "the promise of the Father"?**

This question stems from the following Scriptures:

And, being assembled together with them, (Jesus) commanded them that they should not depart from Jerusalem, but wait for *the promise of the Father*, which, saith he, ye have heard of me.

Acts 1:4

> **Therefore being by the right hand of God exalted, and having received of the Father *the promise of the Holy Ghost*, he hath shed forth this, which ye now see and hear.**
>
> **Acts 2:33**

> **And, behold, I send *the promise of my Father* upon you: but tarry ye in the city of Jerusalem, until ye be endued with power from on high.**
>
> **Luke 24:49**

The key word here is **promise**. God is the Source of all of Jesus' promises; He has the master plan.

God had promised the Holy Spirit in the Old Testament, and Jesus was the completion of that plan. Jesus asked the Father, and the Father sent the Spirit. But the Father would not have sent the Spirit if Jesus had not first come.

The Scriptures do not say that God is the Baptizer. As we have previously learned, this responsibility is reserved for Jesus.

- **Do I have to "tarry" or "wait" to receive the Holy Spirit?**

No. There is no requirement to tarry (or wait) before receiving the baptism of the Holy Spirit.

There are many scriptural accounts of people receiving immediately, and this has been confirmed by today's experiences. However, Jesus expects you to persevere in seeking the baptism.

Jesus appeared to a group of 500 after His resurrection. (1 Cor. 15:6.) Yet on the day of Pentecost, there were only about 120 believers that followed His instructions and faithfully waited for the promise.

Remember, the Holy Spirit was poured out on the earth years ago at Pentecost. You no longer have to wait on the Holy Spirit. You need only to plug into the power by asking in faith.

- **What are some specific methods to "administer" the baptism of the Holy Spirit?**

When we speak of *administering* the baptism, we mean those

actions taken by one person to help another receive the baptism.

After you have received, there is often an eagerness to help others receive this blessing. However, most people are a little confused about where to start.

The following suggestions are for helping others to receive the baptism, but in no way are these meant to be "the *only* way" one can receive. Rather, they are examples recorded in the Bible.

The Laying On of Hands

The Bible speaks of the disciples laying hands upon people for them to receive the baptism of the Holy Spirit.

The laying on of hands does not in any way suggest that the person doing the touching has the power to heal others or has any inherent power of his own. This is only a method to call upon God's power to flow through one person and into another. Touching another person is only an act of obedience and faith, based on the examples set forth in Scripture.

The following Scriptures concentrate on incidents regarding the baptism in the Holy Spirit:

Peter, John and the Samaritans

Now when the apostles which were at Jerusalem heard that Samaria had received the word of God, they sent unto them Peter and John:

Who, when they were come down, prayed for them, that they might receive the Holy Ghost:

(For as yet he was fallen upon none of them: only they were baptized in the name of the Lord Jesus.)

Then *laid they their hands on them, and they received the Holy Ghost.*

Acts 8:14-17

Saul (Paul) and Ananias

We know the apostle Paul (also known as Saul) was filled with the Holy Spirit because he spoke in tongues. In First Corinthians 14:18 he tells us:

I thank my God, I speak with tongues more than ye all.

Here is the account in which a believer (just like you and me) named Ananias was obedient to lay hands on Paul (then called Saul). Then not only was Paul healed, but he was filled with the Holy Spirit:

> **And Ananias went his way, and entered into the house; and *putting his hands on him* said, Brother Saul, the Lord, even Jesus, that appeared unto thee in the way as thou camest, hath sent me, that thou mightest receive thy sight, and be filled with the Holy Ghost.**
>
> **And immediately there fell from his eyes as it had been scales: and he received sight forthwith, and arose, and was baptized.**
>
> Acts 9:17,18

Paul and the Ephesians

> **And it came to pass, that, while Apollos was at Corinth, Paul having passed through the upper coasts came to Ephesus: and finding certain disciples,**
>
> **He said unto them, Have ye received the Holy Ghost since ye believed? And they said unto him, We have not so much as heard whether there be any Holy Ghost.**
>
> **And he said unto them, Unto what then were ye baptized? And they said, Unto John's baptism.**
>
> **Then said Paul, John verily baptized with the baptism of repentance, saying unto the people, that they should believe on him which should come after him, that is, on Christ Jesus.**
>
> **When they heard this, they were baptized in the name of the Lord Jesus.**
>
> **And *when Paul had laid his hands upon them, the Holy Ghost came on them*; and they spake with tongues, and prophesied.**
>
> Acts 19:1-6

Paul and Timothy

The apostle Paul had laid hands on Timothy to receive the Holy Spirit, and he reminds Timothy of it in this Scripture:

Wherefore I put thee in remembrance that thou stir up the gift of God, which is in thee *by the putting on of my hands.*

2 Timothy 1:6

As you can see, the Bible speaks of the disciples laying hands on people and their receiving the Holy Spirit. Not only is there a biblical precedent for this, but it often helps stir up the receiver's faith to receive.

By simply hearing the spoken Word

Peter at the House of Cornelius

While Peter yet spake these words, the Holy Ghost fell on all them *which heard the word.*

And they of the circumcision which believed were astonished, as many as came with Peter, because that on the Gentiles also was poured out the gift of the Holy Ghost.

For they heard them speak with tongues, and magnify God. Then answered Peter,

Can any man forbid water, that these should not be baptized, which have received the Holy Ghost as well as we?

And he commanded them to be baptized in the name of the Lord....

Acts 10:44-48

This event shows the power of the spoken Word of God. It reveals to us the following:

1. God is no respecter of persons (anyone can receive).
2. The Holy Spirit came upon them as a result of Peter's preaching the Word.
3. They spoke in tongues and magnified God.

Through God, without man's help at all

Jesus was with the disciples at the Mount of Olives just before He was taken up in a cloud. At that time, He instructed them to go to Jerusalem, which was about a day's travel away, and to remain there until they received the promise of the Holy Spirit:

> **And, being assembled together with them, commanded them that they should not depart from Jerusalem, but wait for the promise of the Father, which, saith he, ye have heard of me.**
>
> **For John truly baptized with water; but ye shall be baptized with the Holy Ghost not many days hence.**
>
> **...ye shall receive power, after that the Holy Ghost is come upon you: and ye shall be witnesses unto me both in Jerusalem, and in all Judaea, and in Samaria, and unto the uttermost part of the earth.**
>
> **Acts 1:4,5,8**

So they went to Jerusalem and joined together in an upper room. About 120 people were there. (Acts 1:12-15.) On the day of Pentecost God poured out His Spirit in a strong show of power without any human assistance:

> **And when the day of Pentecost was fully come, they were all with one accord in one place.**
>
> **And suddenly there came a sound from heaven as of a rushing mighty wind, and it filled all the house where they were sitting.**
>
> **And there appeared unto them cloven tongues like as of fire, and it sat upon each of them.**
>
> **And they were all filled with the Holy Ghost, and began to speak with other tongues, as the Spirit gave them utterance.**
>
> **Acts 2:1-4**

- **Is there anything else I should know about the baptism?**

  Be prepared for the devil to come against you!

When you receive the baptism in the Holy Spirit, you will become more powerful in the things of God. You will have the power of the Holy Spirit flowing through you, and you will desire to do more for God.

The devil does not want that to happen. He wants to keep God's gift of the Holy Spirit hidden from you. Why? Because with it you will become a stronger enemy to him. After the baptism of the Holy Spirit, you will have more power and will be a more formidable opponent!

You need to understand that the devil will try all of his tricks to keep you from receiving. But just remember, he is the father of lies!

> **Submit yourselves therefore to God. Resist the devil, and he will flee from you.**
>
> **James 4:7**

- **I've received the baptism of the Holy Spirit. Now what?**

Praise the Lord! You have taken a step into a wonderful, deeper relationship with our Lord. The Holy Spirit will function in your life as much as you will allow Him. Remember, you have the ability to either let Him flow through you or quench His works in you.

Now you need to seek the spiritual gifts that are available from Him. As you pray and seek those gifts, they will begin to function in your life as the Holy Spirit gives them to you. The Word says that the Holy Spirit will divide the gifts among you *as He wills*:

> **But all these worketh that one and the selfsame Spirit, dividing to every man severally as he will.**
>
> **1 Corinthians 12:11**

The Holy Spirit will give you a boldness to witness to others. So start telling people about Jesus and share with believers about the baptism of the Holy Spirit!

As you begin to walk forward in this relationship, you will discover all the beautiful promises the Lord has for you.

The baptism in the Holy Spirit and speaking in tongues is not the peak of your walk with Christ but the beginning of a new level of living for Him.

- **After receiving the baptism, is there anything I need to look out for?**

Yes! The devil will try again to steal the Truth from you. Because he has failed to keep you from receiving the baptism, he will come immediately and try to talk you out of it.

As Jesus said in John 10:10, Satan comes **to steal, and to kill, and to destroy** God's blessings. As soon as you receive the baptism of the Holy Spirit, Satan will be there to try to confuse you.

He will try to *steal* your experience away from you, to *kill* the joy that overwhelms you, to *destroy* your faith and the impending spiritual growth.

Here are some of Satan's tactics:

1. He will attempt to convince you that it never happened.
2. He will try to convince you that you made it all up, that it was not from God.
3. He will remind you of your old sins and how "you're just not worthy."
4. He will bring people across your path to belittle your experience.
5. He will attempt to confuse your mind with other problems.
6. He will try to frighten you.
7. He will tell you, "You're making a fool of yourself!"
8. He will even try to make you think he was the one who did it! (He's a glory grabber!)
9. He will attempt to get religion/tradition between you and God.
10. He will try to make you feel uncomfortable or embarrassed about what you believe.

Instead of being deceived by any of his tricks, consider them a confirmation! Satan would not be bothering you if he didn't consider you a threat. And he wouldn't consider you a threat if you weren't getting closer to God and growing spiritually!

In effect, you have initiated a lifelong battle with Satan. But don't lose faith. Your God is big! He is so much more powerful than the devil that it's not even a challenge. If you will continue to follow God and rebuke the devil in Jesus' name, you can't lose!

So don't let the devil talk you out of the blessings of God.

As soon as he comes against you, speak to him like Jesus did. Say, "Get thee behind me, Satan, in the name of Jesus Christ!" or say, "I rebuke you, Satan, in Jesus' name! I bind the spirit of confusion in Jesus' name."

Satan cannot stand up against that kind of warfare!

- **How can I more effectively share with others about the baptism of the Holy Spirit?**

Learn the Word.

Learn the appropriate Scripture verses that support Holy Spirit baptism, so that you may share this truth through God's Word and not by experience alone.

Don't be pushy.

Nobody likes pushy salesmen, no matter how good their product is. First, get to know them, gain their friendship and trust.

Be sensitive to timing.

There are certain times when people will be more receptive. If you blurt out your testimony at an inappropriate time, you may hurt your chances to further pursue that subject with the candidate. Don't let your excitement ruin your witness. God will give you the right opportunity, so wait for it.

Be sensitive to their background.

Nothing will meet more resistance than attacking someone's beliefs or church background. Don't be too aggressive. Don't tell a person to forget everything he has learned in the past and just listen to you. That's *not* an effective way to reach most people.

Find a common ground.

Don't start with your differences. Build on the foundation that person has. Try to relate what he already believes to what you have to tell him. Although denominations vary in many ways, there are often common beliefs on which you can build.

Watch your walk.

If you want to effectively minister the Word of God to someone, it is very important for that person to see God working in your life. I'm not talking about miracles but a simple, obedient Christian walk. You may be very knowledgeable about the Bible and persuasive in speech, but if your walk does not reflect Christ's teachings you will lose credibility.

Be patient!

After you have received the Holy Spirit, there can be such a joy and longing to tell everyone else that you sometimes forget the struggle you yourself went through to believe. It is so exciting that you will want everyone to believe instantly. So don't forget the steps you had to go through in order to believe.

Don't leave God out!

We sometimes get frustrated with newcomers because they are so reluctant to believe. We try everything that we know, but they are still unsure. Remember that it is not up to us to make the change in their lives. That is between them and God. All we are asked to do is to inform them and pray. Let God do His part!

Pray and intercede.

As you pray and intercede on behalf of that individual, God will soften his heart to hear from Him. Then He will let you know the proper timing for approaching that person.

Prayer can change a lot of circumstances. Don't under-utilize it or underestimate its power.

Don't get discouraged.

We are not called to save the world but merely to witness. Jesus will do the saving! You do your part to witness about Jesus, salvation and the baptism of the Holy Spirit. Then let God do His part.

5

Introduction to
The Gifts of the Holy Spirit

In this chapter we will discuss briefly the spiritual gifts and answer some general questions. Then in the next three chapters, we will address in detail each specific gift.

Before beginning this section, you may find it helpful to read First Corinthians, chapters 12-14. This will give you a basic familiarity with the material we will be discussing.

- **What do you mean by "gifts of the Spirit"?**

This refers to the spiritual gifts distributed to individuals after they have received the baptism of the Holy Spirit. These gifts are listed in First Corinthians 12:8-10 as follows:

> For to one is given by the Spirit the word of wisdom; to another the word of knowledge by the same Spirit;
> To another faith by the same Spirit; to another the gifts of healing by the same Spirit;
> To another the working of miracles; to another prophecy; to another discerning of spirits; to another divers kinds of tongues; to another the interpretation of tongues.

These gifts are manifestations of the Holy Spirit. There are nine separate gifts listed in this passage, but God makes it clear that there is only one Spirit.

> Now there are diversities of gifts, but the same Spirit.

And there are differences of administrations, but the same Lord.

And there are diversities of operations, but it is the same God which worketh all in all.

But the manifestation of the Spirit is given to every man to profit withal.

1 Corinthians 12:4-7

The Holy Spirit Himself is in charge of the distribution of these gifts. According to verse 7 above, the manifestation is **given to every man** for the benefit of the whole church body. However, not every person receives the same gift. The Holy Spirit divides these gifts among the people according to His own infinite wisdom.

But all these worketh that one and the selfsame Spirit, dividing to every man severally as he will.

1 Corinthians 12:11

• **How many gifts are there?**

As previously mentioned, there are nine spiritual gifts listed in First Corinthians 12:8-10. These gifts help to bring edification to the church body.

These nine spiritual gifts are:

1. Gift of the word of wisdom
2. Gift of the word of knowledge
•3. Gift of faith
•4. Gifts of healing
5. Gift of the working of miracles
6. Gift of prophecy
•7. Gift of discerning of spirits
8. Gift of divers kinds of tongues
9. Gift of interpretation of tongues

So that you may better understand these gifts, we will discuss each of them in greater detail in the next few chapters. These gifts have been arranged into three groups of three gifts each. These groups will be thoroughly explained and examples will be given.

- **What is the purpose of "spiritual gifts"?**

These spiritual gifts are given to profit the whole Church. They are meant to provide insight and guidance from God through the Holy Spirit.

How much more effective we can be in God's work when we continually apply a portion of His plan that He has shared with us.

The Holy Spirit has given us these gifts in order that we may be edified, each of us profiting from His wisdom. The word *edified* simply means to be built up. In other words, the Holy Spirit builds up our own spirit. Our faith is built up each time we flow in the Spirit.

> **But the manifestation of the Spirit is given to every man to profit withal.**
>
> **1 Corinthians 12:7**

- **What about other gifts like "teaching"?**

First, understand that there are different types of gifts.

The gifts we are studying in this book are the spiritual gifts, also referred to as "gifts of the Spirit" or "Holy Spirit gifts." These gifts have been given by the Holy Spirit to us on an individual basis. Like the Bible says in First Corinthians 12:8, **For to *one* is given by the Spirit....** This indicates that the Holy Spirit does not distribute the gifts in a blanket manner; He gives a certain gift to one individual, and to another He may give a different gift.

The purpose of these spiritual gifts is to bring edification to the whole church body. The individual possessing the gift will also be edified, but that's just a bonus.

The gift of "teaching," which you mentioned, is contained in a separate group of gifts described in the Bible. These gifts are commonly referred to as "ministry gifts." Let's look at this Scripture:

> **And he gave some, apostles; and some, prophets; and some, evangelists; and some, pastors and teachers;**
>
> **For the perfecting of the saints, for the work of the ministry, for the edifying of the body of Christ.**
>
> Ephesians 4:11,12

These ministry gifts are separate from the spiritual gifts as previously listed. Ministry gifts are given to the Church to establish it and help spur it towards maturity.

Another difference is that these ministry gifts are given by Jesus. Just as the Holy Spirit gives the gifts of the Spirit, Jesus gives the ministry gifts. Ephesians 4:11, in speaking of these gifts, says, **And *he* gave...**, referring to Jesus.

In other words, Jesus calls people with certain God-given talents to fulfill the various types of ministry positions. These individuals are gifts to the Church, as Ephesians 4:12 says, **for the perfecting of the saints, for the work of the ministry,** and **for the edifying of the body of Christ.** Other references to these ministry gifts are found in First Corinthians 12:28 and Romans 12:5-8.

This can become confusing, so let me try to clear it up.

The Holy Spirit gives spiritual gifts to individuals to aid them in doing the work of the Lord. This may be shown through a supernatural display of His power or a supernatural word that is used to edify the Church.

The ministry gifts are given by Jesus to guide, educate and mold His Church into maturity.

• **Are the "fruit of the Spirit" the same as the "gifts of the Spirit"?**

No. The term *fruit of the Spirit* refers to those characteristics that are manifested in the lives of Christians as we walk in obedience to Christ.

As we strive to live a life reflecting Jesus Christ, we should show forth certain traits that witness to the change He has made in us. This fruit should be a part of every Christian's life.

The fruit of the Spirit are not supernatural manifestations, like the gifts of the Spirit. They are simply Christlike qualities you will begin to exhibit as you follow a life full of Christ. They are outward manifestations of the inward change that has taken place since you received Jesus.

But the fruit of the Spirit is love, joy, peace, long-suffering, gentleness, goodness, faith,

Meekness, temperance: against such there is no law.

Galatians 5:22,23

• **How do you receive spiritual gifts?**

Spiritual gifts are bestowed upon you by the Holy Spirit Who dwells within you. He has been given the task of dividing up these gifts among God's people. He sees where they are needed to best serve the Lord. But these gifts will be manifested through you only after you have received the baptism of the Holy Spirit.

But all these worketh that one and the selfsame Spirit, dividing to every man severally as he will.

1 Corinthians 12:11

The will of God is known by the Spirit and the Spirit distributes the gifts accordingly.

• **How do you know what gifts you have?**

First, you should *seek* the gifts of the Holy Spirit.

Ask the Holy Spirit to reveal them to you and to manifest Himself through you. As you are faithful in prayer, you will begin to see the gifts manifested in your life. At first, you may be uncertain, but as you step out in faith the Holy Spirit will begin to flow through you.

God wants to use each of us in revealing His Word to the Church. So as we are submissive to the Holy Spirit, we will be used more and more by Him.

Therefore, submit yourself to the Holy Spirit and receive what He has for you. He will clearly reveal to you the nature of your gift(s).

- **Does everyone get every gift?**

Normally no, at least not initially. The Bible says that the gifts are distributed to us by the Holy Spirit **as he will** (1 Cor. 12:11). In other words, He decides which gift(s) to give you.

There are those in the Body of Christ who function in each gift, but generally this is an exception rather than the rule. I have known some of these individuals who have devoted much of their lives to seeking the gifts.

I personally believe it is possible for you to operate in all of the gifts if you pray and seek God about it. However, I also believe you will not be given a gift if you are not ready to effectively handle that gift. The Spirit is wise in distributing these gifts. He places the gifts where He sees the need.

- **Am I qualified to receive spiritual gifts? It seems that only pastors or elders exhibit these gifts.**

This question plagued me in my early understanding of the Holy Spirit. But after I had received the baptism, the Holy Spirit revealed to me the truth that lies beneath this seemingly unfair distribution.

Our spirituality is not measured by the number of gifts operating through our lives. These gifts are manifested *as the Spirit wills*, not necessarily to the most *spiritual* person. The true measure of a person's spirituality is the manifestation of the fruit of the Spirit. How much does he display the Word of God in his own life?

The closer we get to God, the more willing we are to serve Him; and the more willing we are, the more willing He is to use us and bless us. As we do our part, He is always faithful to do His part.

Usually, individuals who are in some form of ministry have spent much time praying and asking for God's will in their lives. In fact, they have likely asked specifically for the gifts of the Holy Spirit to be manifested through them. So by asking, they have received.

The Bible says this over and over, yet we tend to ignore it. Jesus Himself said:

> **If ye abide in me, and my words abide in you, ye shall ask what ye will, and it shall be done unto you.**
> **John 15:7**

> **Ask, and it shall be given you; seek, and ye shall find; knock, and it shall be opened unto you.**
> **Matthew 7:7**

Most people receive not because they ask not!

Be honest. Probably the first time you saw many of the gifts in action from the pulpit, you did not even know they existed! The only difference is that true ministers, elders and other spiritual leaders are committed to God. They spend time with the Lord in prayer and reading the Word. Many times we as laymen do not spend quality time in prayer.

Another thing to remember is that the Holy Spirit gives the gifts to us *as He wills.* This implies that if we are not ready for a particular gift, He will not give it to us at that time. He wants us to have the gifts, but He will not waste them.

- **If the Holy Spirit distributes these gifts, should we still seek them?**

Certainly we should!

Jesus gives us salvation, but before we could get it, didn't we have to seek Him?

Well, Jesus gives us the Holy Spirit, but we have to seek Him too!

The Holy Spirit distributes these gifts in His own wisdom, but if you actively seek the gifts He will faithfully give you a gift.

The apostle Paul, speaking as a mouthpiece of God, said:

But covet earnestly the best gifts: and yet shew I unto you a more excellent way.

1 Corinthians 12:31

God always wants us to have the best. The Holy Spirit is waiting for you to start asking and praying for these gifts. He will be eager to bless you with additional gifts as you continue to grow in Him.

- **If I have one of these gifts, how do I know when to use it?**

There are a variety of ways the Lord may make it known to you. Probably the most common is a simple urging in your spirit, a gentle prompting by the Holy Spirit, to speak forth the word God has given you. You may also hear the message in your mind, then all that's required is for you to simply speak it forth.

I will often hear the message repeated over and over in my mind.

It may be different for you because God works with us as individuals, but when it's God, you know! There will be an inner witness to your spirit.

Sometimes the Holy Spirit wants to see your faith in action. He may give you only the first few words, requiring you to act in faith and begin to speak out before the remainder of the message will come to you. As you say the first words, the rest will follow.

Remember, the Lord is with you. If you become nervous about speaking forth, just know that the Holy Spirit is giving you the words to speak. If working with the Spirit of God isn't a confidence builder, then nothing is!

- **Should we be active in using the gifts?**

Definitely! The whole reason for the Holy Spirit bestowing these gifts upon us is to help us and to profit the church body.

Each of the gifts in its own way is used to promote the power and authority of Christ, and to convince and convict unbelievers. This is why the apostle Paul encouraged Timothy to stir up the gift:

> **Wherefore I put thee in remembrance that thou stir up the gift of God, which is in thee by the putting on of my hands.**
>
> 2 Timothy 1:6

If we each seek the will of God, we will see the importance of spiritual gifts. As more Christians become aware of these gifts and become fluent in their use, the Church as a whole will be strengthened.

These days it is becoming more and more important that we as Christians join together in unity and strength. There is a battle coming soon that will test all of us in our faith. We need every spiritual weapon we can gather.

So put your faith into action and diligently seek your spiritual gifts.

6

The Revelation Gifts

To help you better understand spiritual gifts, they have been divided into three basic categories. Although the Bible does not specifically name any categories, it is helpful that they be grouped together with gifts of similar characteristics.

The first category of gifts we will discuss are *the revelation gifts*, or gifts that reveal things. In other words, these gifts are manifested as revelation of certain events, places, people or situations past and/or present that would not or could not be known by the person through whom the gifts are being manifested.

The three gifts in this category are: (1) the word of knowledge, (2) the word of wisdom and (3) the discerning of spirits.

GIFT OF THE WORD OF KNOWLEDGE

• **Could you give me a brief explanation of this gift?**

The gift of the word of knowledge is the supernatural revealing by God to an individual of certain facts relating to people, places, events and/or situations. This gift always relates to either the present or the past.

There is no such thing as "the gift" of knowledge. It is "the word" of knowledge. This is a word, or a portion, of God's knowledge. He does not give us His full knowledge, just a piece.

The Lord may give you knowledge, and you may be a bright student, but the key to this spiritual gift is *supernatural* knowledge. Above-average intelligence or mental knowledge has no bearing on this gift.

• **Show me some examples of this gift.**

The Samaritan Woman at the Well

Jesus saith unto her, Go, call thy husband, and come hither.

The woman answered and said, I have no husband. Jesus said unto her, Thou hast well said, I have no husband:

For thou hast had five husbands; and he whom thou now hast is not thy husband: in that saidst thou truly.

John 4:16-18

Notice how Jesus supernaturally knew intimate details about this woman whom He had never met. This was a manifestation of the word of knowledge. Jesus knew these three things about her:

1. She indeed did not have a husband (so she was not lying).
2. She had previously had five husbands.
3. She was currently living with a man who was not her husband.

Peter and Cornelius

There was a certain man in Caesarea called Cornelius...,

He saw in a vision...an angel of God...saying unto him, Cornelius.

...send men to Joppa, and call for one Simon, whose surname is Peter:

He...shall tell thee what thou oughtest to do.

While Peter thought on the vision, the Spirit said unto him, Behold, three men seek thee.

Arise therefore, and...go with them, doubting nothing: for I have sent them.

Acts 10:1-6,19,20

The Lord supernaturally revealed to each of these men the existence of the other. He told Cornelius the person to look for and where to find him. Then He told Peter that men were looking for him and he should go with them.

See how wonderfully well the Holy Spirit can function when people are sensitive to Him?

Saul, Samuel and the Lost Donkeys

And Samuel answered Saul, and said....

And as for thine asses that were lost three days ago, set not thy mind on them; for they are found.

1 Samuel 9:19,20

A word of knowledge is not always information about people; it may tell you a variety of facts.

In this story, Saul had been looking for three days for some lost donkeys, so he decided to ask the advice of the prophet Samuel. When Samuel received a word of knowledge about those animals, he was able to assure Saul that they had been found.

Ahijah

And the Lord said unto Ahijah, Behold, the wife of Jeroboam cometh to ask a thing of thee for her son; for he is sick: thus and thus shalt thou say unto her: for it shall be, when she cometh in, that she shall feign herself to be another woman.

And it was so, when Ahijah heard the sound of her feet, as she came in at the door, that he said, Come in, thou wife of Jeroboam; why feignest thou thyself to be another? for I am sent to thee with heavy tidings.

1 Kings 14:5,6

The Lord gave Ahijah a word of knowledge about the identity of the person who would knock on his door, with facts about the woman's plan so he would know what to do. These facts were supernaturally revealed to Ahijah, because he walked with God and functioned in the gifts of the Holy Spirit.

According to verse 4, **Ahijah could not see; for his eyes were set by reason of his age.** So in his own ability Ahijah could not have recognized Jeroboam's wife, and she was disguised so others would not know her. But the word of knowledge operating through Ahijah revealed the truth to him. (See also 1 Kings 19:14-18; 2 Kings 5:20-27; 6:9-12; 1 Sam. 10:22.)

- **If I continue to study the Bible, will I receive this gift?**

Although studying the Scriptures will strengthen your spiritual walk, this is only a method of learning and growing in knowledge. This kind of knowledge should not be confused with the gift of the word of knowledge. As the wording implies, this is a gift.

When referring to the word of knowledge, we do not mean everyday knowledge or textbook knowledge. This knowledge cannot be gathered through some learning process; it is a supernatural knowledge.

You do not earn spiritual gifts through studying or concentrating all your efforts in that particular area. These gifts are given by the Holy Spirit as He wills. In other words, He decides who will get which gift(s).

Don't get me wrong: studying the Scriptures diligently and seeking the Lord in prayer *will* cause your spiritual life to grow. And as a result of this spiritual maturity, the Holy Spirit may decide to bless you with one or more of His gifts. But this does not mean that studying will guarantee that gift.

The Holy Spirit knows your heart, and He knows your spiritual walk. He distributes these gifts to people for His purpose, and only when He decides the time is right. He does not waste gifts. In fact, any believer who has never studied the Bible may just as easily receive a spiritual gift.

In summary, let me say that a person's strong Christian walk does not guarantee his operating in the gifts of the Spirit, but it is the best possible foundation from which those gifts may manifest.

- **How does the gift of the word of knowledge apply to our lives?**

Wonderfully well! The word of knowledge (like all other spiritual gifts) is manifested for the benefit of the believer.

Here the Bible tells us why God gives these gifts:

> **But the manifestation of the Spirit is given to every man *to profit withal*.**
>
> **1 Corinthians 12:7**

This phrase **to profit withal** indicates that these gifts are given to profit everyone!

Remember, this gift of the word of knowledge is a supernatural manifestation, providing you with knowledge from God. This knowledge is often about a situation in your own life, or it may be about something in another person's life. It could be information about an event that is happening or one that has just happened.

As you begin to understand this gift, you will find how useful it truly can be. It can greatly assist you with daily problems and questions, even in knowing how to pray about a particular situation. When you are seeking help on a problem, imagine how great it would be to have God's *knowledge* versus a friend's *opinion*! God never gives you a theory; He gives you the facts!

- **Can a word of knowledge be given to you concerning other people?**

Most definitely. God knows everyone's problems. Since He knows other people's problems as well as your own, He could just as easily give you a word of knowledge concerning situations in their lives.

But God is a wise and loving God. He will not just blab all of their intimate secrets to you. He always has a purpose for a manifestation of His gifts. He does not give them out randomly.

If you receive a word of knowledge regarding another person, it means the Lord desires you to help with that situation. He may have chosen to work through you to assist in that person's problem, but until He gave you that word you didn't know there *was* a problem. At other times, the Lord may simply supply you with information so you will know how to pray for that individual.

In my experiences the Lord has often given me a word of knowledge about a friend or acquaintance so that I could minister to that person. It could be insight regarding a problem he is facing but has not shared with me. If he is unsure about how to proceed in a situation, the Lord may use me to encourage him in the proper direction. At other times I have been given information about a past problem that is still hurting that person in some way.

In each case, the word of knowledge I received regarding another individual was used to encourage, direct and show God's concern for that person.

- **What if you have received a word of knowledge only once; do you still have that gift?**

If it truly was a manifestation of the gift of the word of knowledge, then I would say, yes, you still have that gift.

If an apple tree produces only one apple, we assume it could produce more; that is, if it continues to remain in good condition and obtains proper nourishment.

In the same manner, we can grow dormant in exercising spiritual gifts. If we do not obtain proper spiritual nourishment, we will cease to show fruit.

If you are experiencing this problem, I would suggest that you seek the Lord about it. Pray. Open yourself to Him. Tell Him you desire for Him to work through you, then ask Him to again manifest that gift in your life. There's nothing more pleasing to the Lord than a willing vessel.

- **What is the purpose of the word of knowledge?**

The gift of the word of knowledge has as many uses as God's will requires — infinite! The purpose for all spiritual gifts is to glorify God and to assist the believers in their efforts.

It is impossible to specify all purposes of the word of knowledge, but some of the basic uses for it are:

A. *As a sign to the unbeliever,* as with Jesus and Nathanael. (John 1:45-49.)

B. *To fulfill a task,* as with Ananias and Saul. (Acts 9:10-12.)

C. *To expose a secret sin,* as with Ananias and Sapphira, and the Samaritan woman. (Acts 5:1-5; John 4:16-18.)

D. *To give direction and encouragement,* as when God showed Elijah he was not alone. (1 Kings 19:14-18.)

E. *To glorify God,* as in every case.

GIFT OF THE WORD OF WISDOM

• **Could you give me a brief explanation of this gift?**

The gift of the word of wisdom is a supernatural revealing to an individual of the will and purpose of God. In other words, it reveals either what God is doing, what He is planning to do or what He wants done.

This word of wisdom may simply reveal to you God's purpose, or it may specifically show you an action to take regarding a situation. It gives insight regarding the Lord's purpose for doing certain things or His future plans for people, places, events or situations. The gift of the word of wisdom always relates to *future* things. While the word of knowledge gives you facts, the word of wisdom tells you God's plan of action. Often He tells you how to act on these facts.

There is no spiritual gift called "the gift" of wisdom. Again, this is the gift of "the word" of wisdom.

This word of wisdom is a small portion of the wisdom of God with which He chooses to bless you — just a word, a specific portion of His plan that He desires to share with you.

The Lord may bless you with wisdom — like He did Solomon — but wisdom by itself is not one of the gifts of the Holy Spirit. The Bible says in James 1:5 that if any of us lack wisdom, we may ask for it, and God will provide us with the wisdom we need for our situation. However, that is separate from the gift of the word of wisdom.

Again, the key to this gift is *supernatural* wisdom.

• **Show me some examples of this gift.**

Agabus

And as we tarried there many days, there came down from Judaea a certain prophet, named Agabus.

And when he was come unto us, he took Paul's girdle, and bound his own hands and feet, and said, Thus saith the Holy Ghost, *So shall the Jews at Jerusalem bind the man that owneth this girdle, and shall deliver him into the hands of the Gentiles.*

Acts 21:10,11

This prophet Agabus, who had earlier predicted a great drought (Acts 11:28), was now predicting that Paul would be taken prisoner by the Jews in Jerusalem.

This word of wisdom given to Agabus revealed an event that was to take place in the near future. It obviously was not a known fact, but was a supernatural revelation of the future. This prediction did, in fact, come to pass as described in Acts 21:27-33.

Paul's Ministry

The Holy Spirit was truly active in Paul's life. During his ministry he received many manifestations of the word of wisdom. In each case it was the revelation of a future event and/or a revelation of the will of God for the apostle Paul and his ministry.

While Paul was in Corinth, the Lord had comforted him by giving him the following word of wisdom through a vision:

Then spake the Lord to Paul in the night by a vision, Be not afraid, but speak, and hold not thy peace:

For I am with thee, and no man shall set on thee to hurt thee: for I have much people in this city.

Acts 18:9,10

Then later while in Jerusalem, the apostle Paul was captured and held prisoner. After such an ordeal, it would have been difficult for anyone to proceed with confidence.

Through the years Paul had endured quite a test of his faith. He was beaten, chained, taken prisoner and almost flogged to death with a whip! (See 2 Cor. 11:23-28.)

In Jerusalem he could easily have been questioning what the Lord's next plan was for him. So the Lord encouraged him by giving him a word of wisdom that he would bear witness in Rome:

And the night following the Lord stood by him, and said, Be of good cheer, Paul: for as thou hast testified of me in Jerusalem, so must thou bear witness also at Rome.

Acts 23:11

This, of course, also indicated that he would make it out of Jerusalem alive! Up to that point, Paul had not witnessed in Rome. This is an example of how the Lord used a word of wisdom to relay a future event to encourage a believer.

On another occasion, Paul was given a word of wisdom regarding the ship in which he was sailing. The bad news was:

...Sirs, I perceive that this voyage will be with hurt and much damage, not only of the lading and ship, but also of our lives.

Acts 27:10

Then later came the good news:

And now I exhort you to be of good cheer: for there shall be no loss of any man's life among you, but of the ship.

Acts 27:22

In both revelations, God supernaturally gave Paul information about future events. Why? Because these things were part of God's will and purpose.

It was not God's plan for Paul to be drowned at sea, so He shared this with Paul to encourage him. And the Lord was faithful to His promise — all 276 men on board were saved! (Acts 27:37,44.)

See how comforting it can be to communicate with God?

Guiding, encouraging and comforting the believers, and convincing the unbeliever, are purposes of the Holy Spirit and His gifts. He is our Helper; His mission is to help us talk to God and receive from God. The word of wisdom is one of the gifts that allows God to speak to us.

(See also Gen. 6:12,13; 37:5-9; Joel 2:28; Is. 53.)

- **What is the difference between the two gifts, word of knowledge and word of wisdom?**

The simplest answer is: the word of knowledge is about *facts*, past or present; the word of wisdom refers to the *will* or *purpose* of God in the future.

The word of knowledge gives insight regarding people, places, events or things which either have happened in the past or are happening in the present. The word of wisdom refers to the future (that which has not yet come to pass), either immediate or distant.

Here is another way to look at it: the word of knowledge tells you *what* is happening, the word of wisdom tells you *why* it is happening.

These two gifts can work hand in hand and often can be manifested together. Frequently, a word of wisdom will reveal *how to act* on a word of knowledge.

Let me briefly give some simple definitions of these two words, knowledge and wisdom. Knowledge is the act, fact or state of knowing; in other words, being aware of the facts. Wisdom is *knowing what to do with those facts*.

Once you have the knowledge, you act on it in the future by using wisdom. If you receive a word of knowledge followed by a word of wisdom, then you can know what the problem is and how to deal with it.

Remember, the word of knowledge and the word of wisdom are two separate gifts, just as knowledge and wisdom are different. In worldly terms, many people have knowledge but not all have wisdom. A similar separation exists between these two spiritual gifts.

As an example, suppose during a service I received a word of knowledge that a person who had entered church was carrying a pistol. In the natural, I would be forced to make a decision about how to handle that situation, thinking, *Do I tell an usher? Do I confront that person? Do I call the police?* At that point, all I really know is a fact.

The Lord could also tell me that person does not intend harm. This would be another example of a word of knowledge because it would be a fact. That might be enough for me to make a decision on how to deal with that person.

A word of wisdom would provide direction regarding the situation. It would tell me what to expect and what God's will was in that crisis. The Lord might tell me to walk up to that person and ask him to give me the gun (that would *have* to be the Lord!), or He might have me to pray with that person. We may be reluctant, but God knows what He is doing.

That supernatural wisdom to know the direction to follow is how the gift of the word of wisdom often manifests itself.

• Does the gift of the word of wisdom make you wise?

No. This gift has nothing to do with a person's natural wisdom or the ability to speak wisely. However, when the Lord gives that person a word of wisdom about a situation, he can definitely act wisely.

Many Christians have sufficient knowledge of God's principles to speak wisely to others, but this does not imply that they necessarily have this spiritual gift. The word of wisdom is a supernatural wisdom.

The Lord does not give you wisdom to make *you* wise; He gives you a word of *His* wisdom to minister and build up the Body of Christ.

- **What is the difference between the word of wisdom and prophecy?**

The confusion between these two spiritual gifts is mainly due to an unclear definition of prophecy. The word *prophecy* can be used either specifically or generally.

In a specific sense, prophecy is the gift of prophecy, one of the spiritual gifts to be discussed in a later chapter entitled "The Inspiration Gifts."

In a general sense, prophecy means any prophetic utterance and can include a word of wisdom and/or a word of knowledge. This is why the Old Testament predictions made by prophets are referred to as prophecies.

The gift of word of wisdom is strictly the supernatural revelation of information given by God to an individual. It is manifested internally by that person and does not include a verbalization to the church body.

If the Holy Spirit prompts that person to share that word with the church, then the gift of prophecy is used to perform that function. The gift of prophecy is the supernatural speaking forth of a divinely inspired utterance.

Prophecy is the vocalizing of a message God has given an individual. In our example the message itself would be a word of wisdom. The gift of the word of wisdom is first given to that individual; then through the gift of prophecy, it is given to the church.

When a word of wisdom or word of knowledge is spoken to a church body, we often call it prophecy. But remember, the speaking forth is prophecy.

Prophecy can include a message from the Lord as simple as the words, "I love you." In this case there would be no element of other spiritual gifts. Or, it could include supernatural facts about the future of your church, for example, which would reflect a word of wisdom revealed through the prophecy.

- **How do you receive a word of wisdom or a word of knowledge?**

As with all of God's gifts, only He decides the manner in which to give them. There are no boundaries on God, so He may choose many different ways to manifest His gifts. However, there are a few more common ones, such as:

A. Inward revelation

B. Dreams, as with Joseph

C. Visions (while awake), as with Daniel

D. Special means, as with Ezekiel caught away in the Spirit, John caught up in the Spirit, Gideon spoken to by an angel

The most common way for manifesting these gifts would be through inward revelation; in other words, God revealing the message to you through your spirit and into your mind. You hear, and maybe even see, the words in your own mind. Then by faith you act upon it as is appropriate for the message.

GIFT OF DISCERNING OF SPIRITS

• **Could you give me a brief explanation of this gift?**

The discerning of spirits is a supernatural revelation by God which allows a person to see the presence, activity and intent of a spirit. This includes a revelation regarding the type of spiritual activity that is motivating a particular person.

Discerning of spirits includes both Godly and evil spirits. It also includes a discerning of human spirits, whether evil or good in their intentions.

Let me point out here that there is no such thing as "the gift of discernment," which is mentioned often by some people. The true spiritual gift is the gift of discerning of spirits. This is not thought reading, and it is not the discernment of *things*, like an intuition, but rather the discerning of *spirits*.

Some people who receive knowledge from God about certain facts say they have received "the gift of discernment." This too is incorrect. If what they are describing is indeed the manifestation of one of the spiritual gifts, it is more likely the gift of the word of knowledge.

The gift of discerning of spirits allows you to see into the unseen world and gives revelation regarding the spirit with which you are dealing.

• **Show me some examples of this gift.**

Paul and the Soothsaying Damsel

And it came to pass, as we went to prayer, a certain damsel possessed with a spirit of divination met us, which brought her masters much gain by soothsaying:

The same followed Paul and us, and cried, saying, These men are the servants of the most high God, which shew unto us the way of salvation.

And this did she many days. But Paul, being grieved, turned and said to the spirit, I command thee in the name of Jesus Christ to come out of her. And he came out the same hour.

Acts 16:16-18

Now here is a situation showing how invaluable the Holy Spirit's direction can be. When reading this Scripture, it first appears as if the woman had done nothing wrong. She had announced to everyone that the apostle Paul and company were servants of God. She had even called God **the most high God**, indicating respect and admiration, and she had told the people that this was the way to salvation!

To the general observer, she could have been mistaken for a believer. After many days of following them around, she may have gotten on Paul's nerves, but she still seemed innocent enough.

However, Paul, being filled with the Holy Spirit and functioning in the gift of discerning of spirits, saw something else. The Holy Spirit told him through the discerning of spirits that this woman was not from God, that she was not saying those things as a child of God but as one possessed by an evil spirit. Upon receiving that revelation, the apostle Paul immediately cast out that demon in Jesus' name.

See how invaluable this gift is? Someone may look good on the outside; but through the discerning of spirits, the Holy Spirit can allow you to truly see that person on the inside.

Simon the Soothsayer

And when Simon saw that through laying on of the apostles' hands the Holy Ghost was given, he offered them money,

Saying, Give me also this power, that on whomsoever I lay hands, he may receive the Holy Ghost.

But Peter said unto him, Thy money perish with thee, because thou hast thought that the gift of God may be purchased with money.

Thou hast neither part nor lot in this matter: for thy heart is not right in the sight of God.

Repent therefore of this thy wickedness, and pray God, if perhaps the thought of thine heart may be forgiven thee.

For I perceive that thou art in the gall of bitterness, and in the bond of iniquity.

Acts 8:18-23

Elymas the Sorcerer

And when they had gone through the isle unto Paphos, they found a certain sorcerer, a false prophet, a Jew, whose name was Bar-jesus:

Which was with the deputy of the country, Sergius Paulus, a prudent man; who called for Barnabas and Saul, and desired to hear the word of God.

But Elymas the sorcerer (for so is his name by interpretation) withstood them, seeking to turn away the deputy from the faith.

Then Saul, (who also is called Paul,) filled with the Holy Ghost, set his eyes on him,

And said, O full of all subtilty and all mischief, thou child of the devil, thou enemy of all righteousness, wilt thou not cease to pervert the right ways of the Lord?

Acts 13:6-10

In these two situations, both Peter and Paul used the gift of discerning of spirits to reveal the true spirits behind the individuals and their true purposes.

Again, to the casual observer, those two men — Simon and Elymas — may have looked normal and seemed harmless enough. But the two apostles of God were allowed to see into the spirit realm and to discern the true natures of those men. (See also 2 Kings 6:17; Acts 7:55,56; Is. 6:1.)

- **Does "discerning of spirits" refer only to evil spirits and demons?**

No. As I have previously explained, this gift is the discerning of "spirits," which means *all* spirits, good as well as evil. Now when referring to "good spirits," I do not mean white witches; I mean the Holy Spirit or angels.

True, this gift of discerning of spirits can reveal demonic activity, but that is not its exclusive use.

Through this gift, you are able to see into the spirit realm and determine the type of spirit that is behind a person or situation. This gift not only allows you to see or sense that spirit, but it also gives you knowledge of that spirit's nature, whether it be good or evil.

- **What is discerning of spirits used for?**

In short, discerning of spirits provides critical information to a child of God regarding the spirit that functions behind another individual or situation.

This gift allows us to cut through all the outside layers and get directly to the heart of the matter. We are able to see through all the fake exteriors into the spirit that is behind the person with whom we are dealing.

Primarily this gift is manifested as the believer possessing it has need of it. He may be in a situation where he needs to know the kind of spirit that is at work. Often, during a time of ministry when he is dealing with a person's need, his eyes will be opened to the spirit behind the problem.

This gift may be used to reveal the spirit behind a sickness or disease. It might also be used to choose spiritual men and women for service in God's Church.

- **Would visions be included in discerning of spirits?**

  Certainly! Although some visions might include a word of knowledge or word of wisdom, they definitely would be considered a manifestation of the gift of discerning of spirits.

  A vision is, in effect, a method of seeing into the spirit world. Sometimes during prayer or personal ministry, a believer will receive a vision revealing to him the spirit behind a person or situation. In this way he can specifically address that spirit and more directly deal with the problem.

- **Is mind reading a manifestation of the discerning of spirits?**

  Definitely not! Discerning of spirits is a gift from God and is in no way connected to mind reading, ESP, fortune-telling or any other such things. As a matter of fact, the majority of individuals active in these practices are not even believers.

  You cannot manifest the gifts of God if you have not accepted Jesus Christ as your Savior. Satan has his imitation gifts too.

7

The Power Gifts

The second category of spiritual gifts is known as *the power gifts*. These gifts involve a show of power — not human power but supernatural manifestations of God's power. These gifts consist of action, either on the part of God or the individual.

These power gifts, the special impartation of God's power to an individual, are: (1) the gift of faith, (2) the gifts of healing and (3) the gift of working of miracles.

GIFT OF FAITH

• **Could you give me a brief explanation of this gift?**

With the gift of faith, God brings to pass a supernatural faith, achieving that which is impossible through humans. No human effort is involved.

When you have this gift of faith, God will do the supernatural in your behalf. Such faith will cause you to hold unwaveringly for God's protection or provision of your needs.

• **Show me some examples of this gift.**

There are many examples, but I will share a few, showing clearly how the Lord met people's needs because of the supernatural faith they had.

Daniel in the Lions' Den

My God hath sent his angel, and hath shut the lions' mouths, that they have not hurt me: forasmuch

as before him innocency was found in me; and also before thee, O king, have I done no hurt.

Then was the king exceeding glad for him, and commanded that they should take Daniel up out of the den. So Daniel was taken up out of the den, and no manner of hurt was found upon him, because he believed in his God.

Daniel 6:22,23

Here is an example of a man who manifested the gift of faith in such a way that he was protected from hungry lions! As verse 23 above says, this happened **because he believed in his God.**

It takes a supernatural kind of faith for someone to remain faithful in the midst of a den of lions!

The Hebrew Children in the Fiery Furnace

If it be so, our God whom we serve is able to deliver us from the burning fiery furnace, and he will deliver us out of thine hand, O king.

But if not, be it known unto thee, O king, that we will not serve thy gods, nor worship the golden image which thou hast set up.

Daniel 3:17,18

These Hebrew children — Shadrach, Meshach and Abednego — were immovable believers. They knew that theirs was the only God and that they would never serve another. But when it came time for them to be pitched into a furnace, their true faith was tested!

Though facing disaster, they said they believed that their God would protect them but that, even if He didn't, He was still their God. What a testimony!

As they took those steps into that furnace, the Holy Spirit manifested the gift of faith in their hearts. They were able to endure that punishment without their faith waning.

Elijah and the Ravens

So he (Elijah) **went and did according unto the word of the Lord: for he went and dwelt by the brook Cherith, that is before Jordan.**

And the ravens brought him bread and flesh in the morning, and bread and flesh in the evening; and he drank of the brook.

1 Kings 17:5,6

In this situation, the prophet Elijah was relying on God to supply not only all of his spiritual guidance but also his physical nourishment. He had enough faith to believe that God would use ravens to deliver food to him.

It's hard enough to believe for a supernatural supply, but on top of that, ravens eat meat! How could he believe they would help him? That's like hoping a vulture will leave a dead animal alone. It just doesn't happen! It's their nature to feed on the dead.

But God intervened supernaturally in Elijah's behalf, and his needs were met.

Paul and the Viper

And when Paul had gathered a bundle of sticks, and laid them on the fire, there came a viper out of the heat, and fastened on his hand.

And when the barbarians saw the venomous beast hang on his hand, they said among themselves, No doubt this man is a murderer, whom, though he hath escaped the sea, yet vengeance suffereth not to live.

And he shook off the beast into the fire, and felt no harm.

Howbeit they looked when he should have swollen, or fallen down dead suddenly: but after they had looked a great while, and saw no harm come to him, they changed their minds, and said that he was a god.

Acts 28:3-6

On this occasion, like many others in his life, the apostle Paul manifested the gift of faith. He was not concerned when bit by a viper — he didn't even flinch! He knew the Lord would protect him, but he possessed a supernatural flow of faith to simply shake off that snake and proceed with no thought of needing medical attention.

Now this is not implying that we all should pick up snakes to see if God will work for us! God protects His people when we are *following His will*, but when we get out on our own, we are just playing with fire. The gift of faith must always function under the Holy Spirit's guidance.

We all have faith to varying degrees. Romans 12:3 says, **...God hath dealt to every man the measure of faith.** We would like to say that without even a flinch we would die for our Lord.

But the gift of faith is really more than that. It's a gift from the Lord which allows a person to have faith in something that seems impossible. If it is truly the gift of faith, you won't wonder — you'll know. God will confirm it. (See also 1 Kings 17:13; 2 Kings 6:5,6.)

• **If we all have faith, why then do we need the gift of faith?**

Let's not confuse faith and the gift of faith. There is a difference.

First, there is a type of faith that helps us to accept Christ and receive salvation. This is the normal faith that follows every believer: faith that there really is a God and a Savior.

The gift of faith is different from this normal kind of faith that is exercised by believers. This gift of faith is a supernatural faith. All of the nine spiritual gifts are above and beyond the normal blessings of the Lord.

The gift of faith has a certain element of risk involved and is often associated with life-or-death situations. In these predicaments, normal faith would not be sufficient.

During normal conditions, a loss of faith does not always result in noticeable reverberations. But in a life-or-death situation, there is no room for hesitation.

Daniel experienced a high degree of danger while in the lions' den. Elijah was in a life-or-death situation because he had no food, but the danger with Elijah was not as immediate as with Daniel. Do you see that although very different, both instances contained certain risks involved with trusting the Lord?

- **How does the gift of faith operate?**

The gift of faith opens up the doors of heaven, bringing down all of God's resources upon a situation.

When operating in the gift of faith, your only requirement is to pray and wait upon the Lord. Just as Elijah made no provisions to find his own food, you must simply trust God.

- **Could a person with the gift of faith heal someone else?**

If you are asking whether the gift of faith itself can heal someone, the answer is no. That is not the purpose of this gift.

The purpose of the gift of faith is supernatural protection and/or provision.

Of course, an individual with the gift of faith may also possess the gifts of healing. In that case, the answer to your question would be yes. But then whether that person had the gift of faith would be irrelevant. One gift does not replace another.

- **Didn't it take faith for the disciples to perform miracles?**

Most definitely. But that was not the gift of faith operating through them. They had the same faith that is given to all believers.

The level of faith the disciples had may seem like a special gift, but remember they had many firsthand experiences to build their faith. There is no argument that they had great faith, but much of their faith was the result of their experiences and the function of other spiritual gifts in their lives.

For the most part, these miracles were not manifestations of the gift of faith. The gift of faith was manifested when elements of danger, protection or personal needs were involved.

- **If the gift of faith supernaturally protects you in impossible situations, how does it differ from the gift of working of miracles?**

Here is the best way I know to describe it: the gift of faith allows you to *receive* the miraculous; the gift of working of miracles allows you to *perform* the miraculous through the power of the Holy Spirit.

When operating in the gift of faith, *you* don't do anything; God does everything for you. That's the incredible part! He even gives you the supernatural faith to remain still and calm in impossible situations.

GIFTS OF HEALING

- **Could you give me a brief explanation of this gift?**

The gifts of healing allow you to be used in the supernatural healing of others by the power of the Holy Spirit working through you. It is not *you* that heals; it is the *power of God* flowing through you.

- **Show me some examples of this gift.**

Peter and the Lame Man

Then Peter said, Silver and gold have I none; but such as I have give I thee: In the name of Jesus Christ of Nazareth rise up and walk.

And he took him by the right hand, and lifted him up: and immediately his feet and ankle bones received strength.

Acts 3:6,7

Jesus and Blind Bartimaeus

And Jesus answered and said unto him, What wilt thou that I should do unto thee? The blind man said unto him, Lord, that I might receive my sight.

And Jesus said unto him, Go thy way; thy faith hath made thee whole. And immediately he received his sight, and followed Jesus in the way.

Mark 10:51,52

Jesus and the Woman
Who Touched His Garment

And a woman having an issue of blood twelve years, which had spent all her living upon physicians, neither could be healed of any,

Came behind him, and touched the border of his garment: and immediately her issue of blood stanched.

Luke 8:43,44

Jesus and High Priest's Servant (Malchus)[1]

And one of them smote the servant of the high priest, and cut off his right ear.

And Jesus answered and said, Suffer ye thus far. And he touched his ear, and healed him.

Luke 22:50,51

Paul and Publius's Father

And it came to pass, that the father of Publius lay sick of a fever and of a bloody flux: to whom Paul entered in, and prayed, and laid his hands on him, and healed him.

So when this was done, others also, which had diseases in the island, came, and were healed.

Acts 28:8,9

Elisha and the Shunammite's Son

And when Elisha was come into the house, behold, the child was dead, and laid upon his bed.

He went in therefore, and shut the door upon them twain, and prayed unto the Lord.

And he went up, and lay upon the child, and put his mouth upon his mouth, and his eyes upon his eyes, and his hands upon his hands: and he stretched himself upon the child; and the flesh of the child waxed warm.

Then he returned, and walked in the house to and fro; and went up, and stretched himself upon him; and the child sneezed seven times, and the child opened his eyes.

2 Kings 4:32-35

The gifts of healing are so misunderstood among the nine spiritual gifts. People are as cautious about this gift as about the gift of tongues. Some get nervous whenever this topic is mentioned.

These feelings of fear, nervousness and doubt are a result of the lies we have allowed Satan to feed us through the years. Confusion, due to a lack of knowledge or a lack of openness, has caused many to reject the gifts of healing.

There has been much debate about the legitimacy of healing, and even some frauds have been exposed. However, the sins of these few individuals should not be allowed to shed a bad light upon God's miraculous powers.

It does not matter what you may have heard or seen about healing as being trickery, fake or "of the devil." What does the Word of God have to say about healing? How does the truth of healing manifest itself in the lives of believers? That's what matters!

- **I don't believe anybody can heal people! How can you teach this?**

You're right, a person can't heal anyone — but God can! I understand exactly what you are saying. But don't just look at this on the surface. You need to see the whole picture.

First, I need you to do me a big favor: set aside what you may have heard in the past; let down any walls you have built up. It's just you, me and the Lord, so don't be afraid to step back and take a new look at some things.

Many people have built up resistance to certain subjects, and such is often the case with healing. I know this because at one point I thought the same thing myself! I had to overcome doubt and tradition to open myself to God's truth about healing.

That's why it is important for us to set aside any preconceived notions before we go any farther in this discussion. Over the years people in ministry have been heard saying many things, and much has been seen on television. But for a moment, please put all of that behind you and just listen.

I agree with you to a certain point. I don't believe any person — like you or me — can heal anyone. However, I do believe a person — like you or me — can be used *by God* to heal someone. Can you agree with me on that so far? The Word says:

> **And Jesus looking upon them saith, With men it is impossible, but not with God: for with God all things are possible.**
>
> **Mark 10:27**

Now I will assume that we agree on how God can work through us, so let's look at the next fact. When Jesus sent out His disciples, He gave them the power to heal all manner of sickness and disease:

> **And when he had called unto him his twelve disciples, he gave them power against unclean spirits, to cast them out, and *to heal all manner of sickness and all manner of disease*.**
>
> **...Heal the sick, cleanse the lepers, raise the dead, cast out devils: freely ye have received, freely give.**
>
> **Matthew 10:1,8**

(See also Mark 3:14,15; 16:17,18; Luke 9:1,2; 10:9.)

The book of Acts and other New Testament writings show how the disciples had the power to heal the sick in Jesus' name. These were not just encouraging words He used, but promises and truths regarding their ability to heal the sick. According to God's Word, Jesus Christ is **the same yesterday, and to day, and forever** (Heb. 13:8).

Guess what? God has not forgotten how to make body parts: arms, legs, eyes and eardrums. And He can still do it today!

Why should this be such a remarkable experience for us Christians today? Neither Jesus nor His promises have changed over the years. We have exactly the same blessings, promises and gifts available to us now as the believers had in His day.

In the book of John, Jesus even goes so far as to say that those who believed in Him would do even greater things than He did. So who believes in Him? You and me!

> **Verily, verily, I say unto you, He that believeth on me, the works that I do shall he do also; and greater works than these shall he do; because I go unto my Father.**
>
> **John 14:12**

Did you ever wonder why He added that last phrase **because I go unto my Father**? Nothing in the Bible is just thrown in as a filler. Every word was carefully chosen and placed there by the Holy Spirit. Jesus finished His own statement when He said the following:

> **Nevertheless I tell you the truth; It is expedient for you that I go away: for if I go not away, the Comforter will not come unto you; but if I depart, I will send him unto you.**
>
> **John 16:7**

Can you see it? Jesus said that we would do great things if He went away, because that was the only way for the Spirit to come and manifest in our lives. That was the plan! His sending the Holy Spirit was a completion of God's plan for our lives.

The book of First Corinthians tells us that the Holy Spirit gives spiritual gifts to various individuals. One of those gifts includes healing:

> **...to another the gifts of healing by the same Spirit.**
> 1 Corinthians 12:9

Now let's review the biblical facts in order:

1. With God, all things are possible.
2. Jesus gave His disciples power to heal the sick.
3. The Bible testifies that they did — and that power worked!
4. Jesus said His believers would do greater works than He.
5. We are His believers.
6. Jesus and His promises have not changed over the years.
7. Jesus went to the Father and then sent the Holy Spirit to us.
8. The Holy Spirit gives gifts of healing.

What a glorious plan! God, Jesus and the Holy Spirit always plan things so perfectly. The timing, scheduling and sequence of events are always in order. How could I even begin to teach someone about the gifts of healing if none of these other things had happened?

By looking at this biblical history of events, it is easy to see how the Holy Spirit and spiritual gifts fit into that plan. It's also simple to see how God, through the Holy Spirit, can manifest His healing power today through you and me as believers.

- **If we have the gifts of healing, can we heal everyone? If not, then why not?**

This question has plagued people for generations. There are many different viewpoints, and I will share a few with you, but the bottom line is that God is omnipotent and knows more about the big picture than we do. There are certain things that we cannot possibly understand, so we must in faith leave them with God.

As I promised, I will share with you some biblical insight that we *do* know.

In some instances, disbelief hindered the power of God. Jesus Himself was limited in His works by the unbelief of the people around Him.

> **And he did not many mighty works there because of their unbelief.**
>
> **Matthew 13:58**

> **And he could there do no mighty work, save that he laid his hands upon a few sick folk, and healed them.**
>
> **And he marvelled because of their unbelief. And he went round about the villages, teaching.**
>
> **Mark 6:5,6**

If we are truly seeking to be healed, we must *believe*. If we *don't* have faith and believe, we are putting restrictions on God.

If we *do* take these steps, we should have faith that God will honor His promises.

However, regardless of all these things, there are those that will not be healed.

As Christians this is very frustrating because often the answer is known only by God. The hardest thing for us to understand is that sometimes it is simply God's time to take them home. We tend to fight this concept. We believe God is supposed to be good and love us, and all of that. But when you think of what heaven will be like, isn't it even more loving to take them there than to leave them here?

We will never understand God's mind until we are with Him. The best we can do is to abide by His Word, have faith, and trust in His exceeding wisdom.

- **Is healing dependent upon the faith of the sick person?**

In general, I would say yes.

It is important for the sick person to have faith that the Lord can heal him.

However, while it is *important* for the sick person to have faith that the Lord can heal him, that is not a *requirement* for healing. Read this carefully so you understand that statement.

When Jesus was ministering on earth, there were several circumstances in which a person was healed because of the faith of "others."

For example, the centurion asked the Lord to heal his servant. Jesus did it with a spoken word. The Bible says that the servant was healed even though he was not around to hear Jesus speak. (See Matt. 8:5-13; Luke 7:6-10.) In this instance, the servant was not healed because of his own faith but because of the faith of the centurion.

In another case, a paralytic was brought to Jesus by some friends. Matthew 9:2 says that Jesus, after **seeing *their* faith**, healed him.

So the faith of the sick person is not always necessary for the healing.

My point is that in several instances the sick was not the one who displayed great faith. In many cases, the person being prayed for may not even be conscious or aware of the prayer. But the Lord would not hold back His healing power simply because the sick individual is not cooperating. The Lord respects the faith of the person doing the praying also! (This, of course, does not apply to purposeful rebellion on the part of a sick person.)

If you pray for someone to be healed, do not give up because you think that person's heart may not be in it. Don't underestimate God's faithfulness to answer *your* prayer!

> **Confess your faults one to another, and pray one for another, that ye may be healed. The effectual fervent prayer of a righteous man availeth much.**
>
> **James 5:16**

- **If a sick person is healed after someone else has prayed, does this mean the one who prayed has the gifts of healing?**

Not necessarily. Not every healing is a manifestation of the gifts of healing. The Lord is faithful to answer our prayers for healing just like He answers other prayers. The gifts of healing operate above and beyond that type of healing.

The gifts of healing are manifested in the lives of certain individuals who are given this gift specifically to allow God's power to be shown. Generally speaking, the individual possessing this gift will show many manifestations of healings throughout his lifetime. Like with the other gifts, the Holy Spirit distributes the gifts of healing as He chooses.

• **Do the gifts of healing include "raising the dead"?**

My personal belief is that the raising of the dead is actually a manifestation of two gifts: the gift of working of miracles and the gifts of healing.

Obviously, it is a miracle whenever a person is raised from the dead, but that person must also be healed of what killed him in the first place! If not, he might again die as a result of that same disease, injury, affliction or other adversity. For example, if an individual died from a diseased heart, God could perform the miracle of raising from the dead simply by breathing life into him. However, God must also heal that diseased heart.

• **Do the gifts of healing include "casting out demons"?**

Specifically, no. The Bible distinguishes between these two. Healing and casting out demons are stated as separate entities:

> **And he ordained twelve, that they should be with him, and that he might send them forth to preach,**
>
> **And to have power to heal sicknesses, and to cast out devils.**
>
> **Mark 3:14,15**

Casting out devils is not exclusively associated with any of the nine spiritual gifts. However, in a given instance, several of these gifts could be involved.

The confusion is that often the casting out of demons will manifest an apparent healing. In many instances, Jesus encountered individuals who had certain spirits which caused physical diseases or problems. Here are two of these confrontations:

Then was brought unto him one possessed with a devil, blind, and dumb: and he healed him, insomuch that the blind and dumb both spake and saw.

Matthew 12:22

And as he was yet a coming, the devil threw him down, and tare him. And Jesus rebuked the unclean spirit, and healed the child, and delivered him again to his father.

Luke 9:42

In these situations there was not so much the healing of a disease as the release of a demon. Jesus tells us:

And these signs shall follow them that believe; In my name shall they cast out devils; they shall speak with new tongues.

Mark 16:17

(See also Matt. 10:8; Mark 3:15.)

• **When did someone besides Jesus exhibit the gifts of healing?**

Many, many times. The Bible does not specifically follow the lives of every believer, but it does give us a few examples of believers who exhibited the gifts of healing.

The apostle Peter, for example, had many healings and miracles during his life, but some people don't identify with him because he was one of the twelve disciples. People tend to put too much emphasis on the disciples as being special and having special powers because they had walked with Jesus.

True, their walk with Jesus gave them the power, but so does *our* walk with Him — through the power of the Holy Spirit!

To help your faith, I have pointed out below some individuals who were not "disciples," as were the Twelve. They were just believers like you and me!

We often forget that the apostle Paul was not one of "the Twelve." Even if you feel that these Twelve were given certain special gifts, you have to agree that Paul was really no different than you or me.

Here are just a few of the many references to stories as recorded in the book of Acts:

THE BOOK OF ACTS

PAUL	PETER	APOSTLES	PHILIP	ANANIAS
14:8-10	3:1-8	5:12-16	8:5-7	9:17,18
16:16-18	9:33,34			
19:11,12	9:36-41			
20:7-12				
28:8				

- **Is touching the sick person a requirement for healing?**

No, it is not always necessary to touch the sick person for him to be healed. If we look at the Scriptures, we will find that many of these healings were done by a spoken word, a command or an action by the sick person.

However, in Mark 16:17,18 Jesus said that certain signs would follow those who believe in Him. One of these signs involves touching the sick. He said that when we lay hands on the sick in His Name they would recover.

Also, James 5:14 says that one who is sick should call on the elders of the church and be anointed with oil (which requires touching), and the sick person would be made well.

This is biblical truth, and I am not contesting that point, but you asked if touching is a requirement for healing. In the context of your question, I would have to say no. It is a helpful instruction to the Church, but it is not a law.

If you are sick or hurting, first pray for yourself and believe for your healing. But there is nothing wrong with having someone else to pray with you. Remember, the laying on of hands is an act of obedience and faith in God's Word. So don't be offended or frightened if someone who is praying for you wants to lay hands on you when he prays. That is scriptural.

• **Do you believe in the laying on of hands?**

Yes, I believe in this because it is scriptural. Of course, this is assuming it is done while praying for an individual.

Sometimes people will join hands or touch while praying. This form of touching is merely a sign of unity. It shows that they are joining together in one accord to lift up their prayers to the Lord.

The laying on of hands is a more definite, conscious effort to place your hands upon a person while praying for him.

Many people have a negative attitude regarding this. I've heard people whisper, *They believe in laying on of hands!* They say it like it's some sort of crazy ritual.

Let me say one more time: it is scriptural. Jesus said we are to do it! If done in a proper spirit of worship and prayer, it is positively legitimate in the eyes of God.

A ruler of the synagogue fell at Jesus' feet and said:

...**My little daughter lieth at the point of death: I pray thee, come and lay thy hands on her, that she may be healed; and she shall live.**

Mark 5:23

When Jesus gave authority to His disciples, He said:

...**they shall lay hands on the sick, and they shall recover.**

Mark 16:18

(See also Acts 8:19.)

• **How are healings performed?**

For an example of the ways healings are performed, we can look at the life of Jesus. Here are several ways the Bible shows that healings occurred during His ministry:

Through a *spoken word* (spoken either softly or as a command)

2. Through a *touch*
3. Through an *action* by the person desiring to be healed
4. Through an *action* by the person ministering healing

The methods Jesus used were examples for us, and nothing has changed through the years.

Today the exact technique you follow in each situation you face will be revealed to you by the Holy Spirit. It may be one of these methods, or it could be a combination. It might even be something not found on this list. The important thing is for you to follow the leading of the Holy Spirit. He will help you to know the proper procedures at the proper time.

- **Why are "the gifts of healing" the only gift in the plural form?**

There are several theories about this. The theory which seems to have the most merit contends that the plural aspect refers to the healing of different types of sickness and disease. In other words, the *"gifts* of healing" would be for healing various conditions, such as arthritis, cancer, blindness or deafness.

This has merit because many well-known ministers, evangelists and missionaries have shown this gift for healing a particular type of sickness or disease.

- **Isn't healing also considered a miracle?**

Yes, it is a miracle in the basic definition of the word, but it is not the gift of working of miracles.

The level of sickness or disease that is conquered does not have any bearing on whether it is classified a miracle. Events occur almost daily that would be considered miraculous. When a baby survives a deadly car crash or a pilot survives a plane crash, we consider those miracles. But they do not involve a specific individual operating in a spiritual gift.

The gift of working of miracles is manifested through an individual who possesses that gift.

- **Is prayer always necessary for the gifts of healing to manifest?**

Anyone who has received the gifts of healing is most certainly involved in a steady prayer life. Generally, anyone expecting to encounter a sick person will have prayed over that situation for God to answer his prayers.

But there are instances in which people have been healed without a specific prayer from the person possessing the gifts of healing. Two instances in the Bible come to mind:

Jesus and the Woman
Who Touched His Garment

And a woman having an issue of blood twelve years, which had spent all her living upon physicians, neither could be healed of any,

Came behind him, and touched the border of his garment: and immediately her issue of blood stanched.

Luke 8:43,44

Peter and his Shadow

Insomuch that they brought forth the sick into the streets, and laid them on beds and couches, that at the least the shadow of Peter passing by might overshadow some of them.

There came also a multitude out of the cities round about unto Jerusalem, bringing sick folks, and them which were vexed with unclean spirits: and they were healed every one.

Acts 5:15,16

In these two situations, both Jesus and Peter were unaware of the individuals who sought healing. They were therefore unprepared for specific prayers. Nonetheless, all received the healings they sought.

That is the faithfulness of God in manifesting His gifts.

- **If I am sick, should I go to the doctor; and if I do, is that showing a lack of faith in God?**

When you begin to feel sickness, the first thing you should do is to pray for your healing. Without a doubt, the Lord is able to heal you of any sickness or disease that might attack you.

But remember to pray the prayer of faith! Faith can move mountains or heal sickness! God will work according to the proportion of your faith.

Remember, however, the Lord manifests healings in a variety of ways. Sometimes it is immediate and sometimes it comes through the help of a doctor. God believes in doctors too! Even Luke, one of Jesus' followers, was a physician. The Lord gives doctors and nurses a special desire to help other people, and He honors their willingness to minister to them.

Now don't get me wrong, your best medicine by far is still prayer. But the Lord did not make us ignorant; He gave us common sense to make decisions. We should not use doctors and hospitals as a crutch for our faith, but neither should we lose sight of reality. Sickness will try to come against us — there is no ignoring that fact — but victory over sickness is also a promise from the Lord.

The best procedure is to pray a prayer for healing, mix it with faith and then believe God for healing.

I have seen God answer that prayer through supernatural healing, and I have seen Him answer it through the skillful hand of a surgeon. If the sickness is removed, can you say that one was more an answer to prayer than the other?

GIFT OF WORKING OF MIRACLES

- **Could you give me a brief explanation of this gift?**

The gift of working of miracles allows you to perform supernatural acts of wonder through the power of the Holy Spirit.

Now some healings will be considered miracles, and vice versa, but these are two separate gifts. Also, there is no "gift of miracles"; it is the "working of miracles."

• **Show me some examples of this gift.**

Paul and Elymas

But Elymas the sorcerer (for so is his name by interpretation) withstood them, seeking to turn away the deputy from the faith.

Then Saul, (who also is called Paul,) filled with the Holy Ghost, set his eyes on him,

And said, O full of all subtilty and all mischief, thou child of the devil, thou enemy of all righteousness, wilt thou not cease to pervert the right ways of the Lord?

And now, behold, the hand of the Lord is upon thee, and thou shalt be blind, not seeing the sun for a season. And immediately there fell on him a mist and a darkness; and he went about seeking some to lead him by the hand.

Then the deputy, when he saw what was done, believed, being astonished at the doctrine of the Lord.

Acts 13:8-12

This Scripture shows that the apostle Paul was filled with the Holy Ghost and spoke this miracle into existence. Through the power of the Holy Ghost, he miraculously blinded this evil man for a season. As with all of the spiritual gifts, the Lord was magnified and the deputy who saw it believed.

Jesus and the Wedding Feast

And there were set there six waterpots of stone, after the manner of the purifying of the Jews, containing two or three firkins apiece.

Jesus saith unto them, Fill the waterpots with water. And they filled them up to the brim.

And he saith unto them, Draw out now, and bear unto the governor of the feast. And they bare it.

When the ruler of the feast had tasted the water that was made wine....

John 2:6-9

This is the story of Jesus' first miracle: turning water into wine when the wedding party had run out of it. John 2:11 confirms that this was the first miracle Jesus performed.

If you begin reading in John 1:29, you will see that this first miracle occurred *after* Jesus had received the Holy Spirit at His water baptism. (John 1:32,33.) This is another testimony to the fact that the Holy Spirit is the Giver of spiritual gifts. Jesus came to earth as a man; and like other men, He needed the power of the Holy Spirit before He could begin His ministry. He was thirty years old (Luke 3:23) and had yet performed no miracles.

Jesus and the Fig Tree

And seeing a fig tree afar off having leaves, he came, if haply he might find any thing thereon: and when he came to it, he found nothing but leaves; for the time of figs was not yet.

And Jesus answered and said unto it, No man eat fruit of thee hereafter for ever. And his disciples heard it.

And in the morning, as they passed by, they saw the fig tree dried up from the roots.

And Peter calling to remembrance saith unto him, Master, behold, the fig tree which thou cursedst is withered away.

And Jesus answering saith unto them, Have faith in God.

Mark 11:13,14,20-22

Jesus miraculously withered this fig tree. At first glance it seems to be an act of anger or a waste. But if you read the rest of the chapter you will find that this was a faith builder for the disciples.

Jesus Calms the Storm

And he arose, and rebuked the wind, and said unto the sea, Peace, be still. And the wind ceased, and there was a great calm.

Mark 4:39

You see, a person's actions may not be anything spectacular, but the results of those actions are!

Jesus only *spoke* to the wind and sea, yet they miraculously calmed.

The gift of working of miracles uses an *ordinary* person to create an *extraordinary* event.

(See also Judg. 14:5,6; 2 Kings 2:8; Matt. 14:19-21; John 6:19.)

* **What is the difference between a "miracle" and the "gift of working of miracles"?**

The difference is that an individual with the gift of working of miracles is involved.

God performs some miracles on His own, and these are not always manifested through people. But the gift of working of miracles involves the action of the individual possessing that gift. There is a difference.

Suppose a major earthquake caused a building to collapse while someone was inside. If the person escaped unharmed, we would call that a miracle.

However, suppose during the middle of the earthquake that person said, "Earth, shake no more!" and the earthquake instantly stopped. Now that would be the gift of working of miracles!

The gift of working of miracles is manifested through a person, not a circumstance.

* **What is the purpose of the gift of working of miracles?**

Like all of the spiritual gifts, it is difficult to narrow the purpose of God into a few simple words. However, all of these gifts serve to glorify God in some way.

The gift of working of miracles serves to give evidence of God's Presence, to confirm the Lord's Word or to confirm the divine calling of a specific individual.

* **Are all miracles manifested as healings?**

No. Many miracles performed in the Bible had nothing to do with healing. Jesus walked on the water. He calmed the sea.

He withered the fig tree. He fed thousands with a few fish and a few pieces of bread.

Other miracles that were not healings, as documented in the Bible, were accomplished by the disciples and Old Testament men, such as Moses.

Often, the laws of nature are superseded by the working of miracles, such as with the parting of the Red Sea or the plagues of Egypt.

If miracles and healings were the same, the Lord would not have listed them separately.

Miracles demonstrate the *power* of God, while healings demonstrate the *compassion* of God.

• Are all miracles outward signs, or can they be less visible?

In observing the miracles of the Lord as shown in the Bible, I would have to say that they must be outwardly visible. The whole reason for the gift of working of miracles is to demonstrate God's power as a sign or confirmation to those who are watching.

If, for example, a person was healed of internal cancer, this would be considered healing and not the working of miracles. If a person accepted salvation after many years of being prayed for by someone else, this would seem miraculous, but it would not be a manifestation of the working of miracles. Both of these are inward signs.

But when Jesus calmed the sea, that was the gift of working of miracles. It was visible to everyone involved, and it clearly showed the power of God.

• Do the Old Testament miracles also fall under this category?

Yes, all those Old Testament miracles were performed through the power of God.

Now we are considering only the miracles that involved men. For instance, God's creation of the earth would be considered a miracle, not the gift of working of miracles. This gift must involve the Lord working through a person, not just the Lord working on His own. It can't be a *gift* if the Holy Spirit has not *given* it to anyone!

Before Christ came, the Holy Spirit was given to certain men for special tasks. These "Spirit-filled" men performed many miracles through the power of the Holy Spirit.

---

[1] In John 18:10 this servant is named Malchus.

8

The Inspiration Gifts

The third category of spiritual gifts is known as *the inspiration gifts.*

The inspiration gifts are provided to strengthen the Church and bring edification, encouragement and comfort. These gifts are: (1) the gift of prophecy, (2) divers kinds of tongues and (3) interpretation of tongues.

GIFT OF PROPHECY

• **Could you give me a brief explanation of this gift?**

The gift of prophecy is the speaking forth of a message from God in a natural language. As God supernaturally gives a message to someone, He also gives that person the ability to express it.

This gift of prophecy is always used to edify, encourage and comfort the Church. This could, of course, be for any body of believers. One might call it a supernatural utterance in a *known* tongue.

The Hebrew word for *prophesy* means "to speak by inspiration."[1] So, in effect, when prophesying you are God's spokesperson! That means you are speaking forth God's Word!

Prophecy does not mean foretelling the future. That is associated with the revelation gifts, specifically the word of wisdom. Instead, prophecy is "forth telling," or telling forth God's Word.

• **Show me some examples of this gift.**

Zacharias, John the Baptist's Father

And his father Zacharias was filled with the Holy Ghost, and prophesied, saying,
Blessed be the Lord God of Israel; for he hath visited and redeemed his people.

Luke 1:67,68

In this story many people were standing around when Zacharias prophesied an encouraging message to them. He said that God was to be blessed for He had visited His people through the blessing of a child and had redeemed them.

The message Zacharias spoke lifted the spirits of those around him. He had *prophesied* by speaking forth that word which the Holy Spirit had revealed to him.

Elisabeth, John the Baptist's Mother

First, a little background...

An angel appeared to Mary, who was to be the mother of Jesus. He told her that the Holy Spirit would come upon her and she would give birth to the Savior. Immediately she went to tell her cousin Elisabeth about this glorious event.

Since there were no phones in those days, Elisabeth had not heard the news. But as soon as Mary greeted her, the reaction was immediate:

And it came to pass, that, when Elisabeth heard the salutation of Mary, the babe leaped in her womb; and Elisabeth was filled with the Holy Ghost:

And she spake out with a loud voice, and said, *Blessed art thou among women, and blessed is the fruit of thy womb.*

Luke 1:41,42

This is an example of the gift of prophecy in conjunction with the gift of the word of knowledge.

Notice that Elisabeth **spake out with a loud voice**. This was a prophetic utterance of what God had told her. The message itself told how Mary and her baby were blessed. At that time, only Mary knew she was carrying a child, but the Holy Spirit revealed it to Elisabeth through a word of knowledge. This word spoken forth was a comfort and encouragement to Mary.

If you have ever had a supernatural experience with God, the whole concept can be mind boggling. You can be positive that it happened, but it can be so wonderful that it's hard to believe it's real!

It would be like winning a million dollars. With that check placed in your hand, you still wonder if you will suddenly wake up!

The same was probably true with that young, innocent girl named Mary. And then her cousin greets her with a confirmation like that! Wow!

That would strengthen anyone's faith. This is the type of encouragement and comfort that comes from being faithful to speak forth the gift of prophecy.

- **What is the purpose of the gift of prophecy?**

The gift of prophecy is a method by which God uses us to speak forth His message for the Church.

The Bible gives us three specific reasons for this spiritual gift:

> **But he that prophesieth speaketh unto men to edification, and exhortation, and comfort.**
> **1 Corinthians 14:3**

Edification means an upbuilding, or in other words, a spiritual strengthening.

Exhortation means an encouragement. A prophecy might be a word of encouragement to the Body.

Comfort is that which it indicates: a gentle, comforting word.

If you encounter a prophecy that does not fit one of these three categories, then either it is not a prophecy or it is not from God.

- **Isn't prophecy telling the future?**

This is a common misunderstanding regarding prophecy. In the Old Testament, there were prophets who told of forthcoming events. An example would be Joel foretelling the pouring out of the Holy Spirit on all mankind. God spoke through him, saying:

> **And it shall come to pass afterward, that I will pour out my spirit upon all flesh; and your sons and your daughters shall prophesy, your old men shall dream dreams, your young men shall see visions.**
>
> **Joel 2:28**

These Old Testament prophets spoke forth the wonderful things of God as a testimony to the people. Often included in those messages was the gift of the word of wisdom. This is where the future comes in. Whatever the message might have been, the prophets spoke it forth through the gift of prophecy.

Specifically speaking, the gift of prophecy refers to *"forth telling,"* not *fore*telling. Today, this is usually manifested as a *telling forth* of God's Word in a church setting — a supernatural "forth telling." That is, God gives an individual a message which He wants to share with His people. This gift of prophecy is not in tongues, but in a natural language.

- **Does the gift of prophecy enable you to predict things?**

Again, the gift of prophecy is not connected with predictions or a foretelling of the future. This gift is defined as the simplest inspired utterance. Look again at what the Word says about prophecy:

> **But he that prophesieth speaketh unto men to edification, and exhortation, and comfort.**
>
> **1 Corinthians 14:3**

> **Now, brethren, if I come unto you speaking with tongues, what shall I profit you, except I shall speak to**

you either by revelation, or by knowledge, or by prophesying, or by doctrine?

1 Corinthians 14:6

Notice in this first Scripture that neither revelation nor predicting the future is mentioned. In the second Scripture, revelation is mentioned as separate and distinct from prophesying. We get confused sometimes because of the liberty with which this word is used. Let me try to explain.

Prophecy can be defined as any inspired utterance. This could be words as simple as, "I am the Lord, and I am watching over you." If the Lord were to give that message to someone, that person would speak it forth through the gift of prophecy for an entire church to hear.

This is not a supernatural revelation of facts known to God, as in a word of knowledge. Nor is it a supernatural revelation of facts as to the will of God. It is simply a supernatural message the Lord wants given to His people. As always, it would produce edification, encouragement and comfort.

Some of these utterances could possibly speak of future events. However, the content of the message is not what makes it a prophecy (other than meeting the qualifications of edification, encouragement, comfort); the content could be a word of wisdom or a word of knowledge. The gift of prophecy refers only to the speaking forth of God's Word.

God may reveal to you a word of wisdom for His Body. To transmit that message to the Body, you would use the gift of prophecy.

Prophesying is speaking forth a word from God through supernatural prompting. That word could be a simple statement of God's love, or it could be a word of wisdom or a word of knowledge which God has given us. All that is required of us is to simply speak it forth in faith.

Prophecy — Like a Cup of Coffee

Let's consider another analogy.

Picture the gift of prophecy as a *cup of coffee*. (This may sound weird, but trust me.) Now, imagine the gift of the word of knowledge as *sugar* and the gift of the word of wisdom as *cream*.

If I gave you a cup of coffee, a cup of sugar and a cup of cream, you could easily distinguish between the three. But if I mixed the sugar or cream in the coffee, it would be more difficult to recognize. More importantly, even if I add sugar or cream to the coffee, it is still called coffee. Right? (Now stay with me, and don't forget those ingredients.)

When I give you the coffee, you can see if there is cream in it, but to you it's still basically just a cup of coffee. You don't concentrate on the cream so as to call it a cup of cream, nor do you assume that all coffee has cream.

Now, let's move our example to church.

When I prophesy (present the *coffee*) in church, it may contain a word of wisdom (*cream*), and all that the church hears is the prediction part (the *cream*). They concentrate on the content, and not the medium.

So what happens? They mix the two together and begin to assume that *all coffee has cream* (or all prophecy has prediction). If the prophecy (the *coffee*) had contained only a word of knowledge (*sugar*), then there would have been no prediction at all!

Remember, the gift of prophecy is a supernaturally inspired utterance, which may or may not contain a revelation of future events. Hopefully, this helps to clarify the purpose and use of this gift of prophecy. If not, have a cup of coffee and think about it!

- **Does having the gift of prophecy make you a prophet?**

Specifically, no. Don't get *prophet* and *prophecy* confused. The prophet is one of the five ministry gifts given to the Church.

> **And he gave some, apostles; and some, prophets; and some, evangelists; and some, pastors and teachers;**
> **For the perfecting of the saints, for the work of the ministry, for the edifying of the body of Christ.**
> **Ephesians 4:11**

Any individual holding one of these offices — not just the prophet — could have the gift of prophecy. In fact, any believer may possess the gift of prophecy.

The gifts of the Holy Spirit are separate from the ministry gifts. However, a person holding the office of prophet will often have the spiritual gifts described in these chapters. Thus, through the revelation gifts, he is often known for telling of future events.

By design, a prophet will have the gift of prophecy, but not everyone having the gift of prophecy is a prophet.

For example, a surgeon would naturally have the tools of a surgeon, such as a scalpel. However, if I have a scalpel, that alone does not make me a surgeon. And it would be wrong for me to claim myself as such.

DIVERS KINDS OF TONGUES

• **Could you give me a brief explanation of this gift?**

In the gift of divers kinds of tongues, God supernaturally gives words in an unknown tongue, which when accompanied by the interpretation will bring edification to the Body. In short, this gift is a message from God manifested in a language unknown by the speaker.

The word *divers* simply means "various."[2] In other words, the gift of tongues is manifested in many various kinds of unknown languages. Everyone does not receive the same language.

• **Show me some examples of this gift.**

The Believers at Pentecost

And they were all filled with the Holy Ghost, and began to speak with other tongues, as the Spirit gave them utterance.

And there were dwelling at Jerusalem Jews, devout men, out of every nation under heaven.

> **Now when this was noised abroad, the multitude came together, and were confounded, because that every man heard them speak in his own language.**
>
> **Acts 2:4-6**

Not only did the disciples and other believers speak in divers kinds of tongues, but all the people around heard the message in their own languages! The Scriptures describe those present as **men, out of every nation under heaven!** The disciples could not have known all those languages. In this case, God supernaturally provided the interpretation to each hearer.

- **Is the gift of speaking in tongues the same as the initial sign of speaking in tongues?**

In a general sense, yes; in a specific sense, no. Let me explain.

In the general sense, speaking in tongues is the same, no matter what the setting. Your spiritual language is given in the same manner, whether you are at home in your prayer time or at church. There is nothing different about the actual tongues. In either case, it is the Holy Spirit supernaturally prompting you with the words to say.

The distinction is that the *gift* of divers kinds of tongues refers to a special gift the Holy Spirit bestows upon some individuals. This gift is used in a church or group setting in order to edify the church body.

The difference between your prayer language and this gift is not in the speaking but in the setting. When you pray in tongues privately, you are speaking to God. When you deliver a message in tongues, God is talking to those people.

- **Why do we need the gift of tongues? We already have tongues and prophecy!**

The main reason is that the gift of tongues *when accompanied by an interpretation* will edify the whole Church!

> **I would that ye all spake with tongues, but rather that ye prophesied: for greater is he that prophesieth**

than he that speaketh with tongues, *except he interpret*, that the church may receive edifying.

1 Corinthians 14:5

- ## What about all of the Scriptures that speak against tongues?

Actually, *there are no* Scriptures that speak against tongues. Most of the confusion comes from Paul's letter to the church in Corinth. Paul was responding to their request for guidance regarding some confusion in the Church.

Specifically, in chapter 14 Paul focuses on the differences between prophecy and speaking in tongues.

> **For he that speaketh in an unknown tongue speaketh not unto men, but unto God: for no man understandeth him; howbeit in the spirit he speaketh mysteries.**
>
> **But he that prophesieth speaketh unto men to edification, and exhortation, and comfort.**
>
> **He that speaketh in an unknown tongue edifieth himself; but he that prophesieth edifieth the church.**
>
> **I would that ye all spake with tongues, but rather that ye prophesied: for greater is he that prophesieth than he that speaketh with tongues, except he interpret, that the church may receive edifying.**
>
> **1 Corinthians 14:1-5**

In these first five verses, Paul compares prophecy to speaking in tongues *without an interpretation*. His emphasis is not the importance of prophecy or tongues, but the edification to the church body.

He is explaining to the Corinthians that a message in tongues for the congregation is not edifying in the church *unless there is an interpretation*. The gift of tongues and interpretation of tongues must work together in a church setting.

Keep in mind that this discussion about tongues does nor refer to your private prayer language but to the gift of tongues used in a corporate setting with the companion gift of interpretation.

In verse 19, Paul reiterates the importance of teaching others:

> **Yet in the church I had rather speak five words with my understanding, that by my voice I might teach others also, than ten thousand words in an unknown tongue.**
>
> **1 Corinthians 14:19**

Again, the emphasis is on a message in tongues that is *not* interpreted. Without interpretation, the message would not help the church learn.

Then Paul has to deal with some disorderly conduct. The Corinthians weren't sure how to use the gifts and were obviously talking over one another.

> **How is it then, brethren? when ye come together, every one of you hath a psalm, hath a doctrine, hath a tongue, hath a revelation, hath an interpretation. Let all things be done unto edifying.**
> **If any man speak in an unknown tongue, let it be by two, or at the most by three, and that by course; and let one interpret.**
> **But if there be no interpreter, let him keep silence in the church; and let him speak to himself, and to God.**
>
> **1 Corinthians 14:26-28**

Paul was not downplaying tongues, but simply restoring order to the chaos. Through the Holy Spirit's revelation, he lays down the proper etiquette for sharing the gifts.

These boundaries, of course, refer only to the gift of tongues as used in a corporate worship environment, not your private prayer language. In your private prayer life, you are talking to God, not men, so there is no need for interpretation.

God always does things in an orderly fashion. He will always choose the method that will most efficiently convey His message to the Church. He would not want everyone talking at once. This would be confusing and would interfere with His message.

> **For God is not the author of confusion, but of peace, as in all churches of the saints.**
> **Let all things be done decently and in order.**
> **1 Corinthians 14:33,40**

Now that we've got all the correction over with, let's look at the positive side of Paul's instructions.

For a balanced prayer life, Paul encourages us to pray with the Spirit (pray in tongues), and also in our understanding (native language). He also encourages singing in the Spirit (sing in tongues) and our understanding.

> **What is it then? I will pray with the spirit, and I will pray with the understanding also: I will sing with the spirit, and I will sing with the understanding also.**
> **1 Corinthians 14:15**

Too many people use this chapter to indicate that we should not speak in tongues. But it is simply a list of instructions to new Christians on how to use the gifts. Here are three Scriptures that clearly show Paul's feelings about tongues:

> **I thank my God, I speak with tongues more than ye all.**
> **1 Corinthians 14:18**

> **I would that ye all spake with tongues....**
> **1 Corinthians 14:5**

> **Wherefore, brethren, covet to prophesy, and forbid not to speak with tongues.**
> **1 Corinthians 14:39**

Here is a summary of Paul's response to the issue:

1. Seek the gift of prophecy because it is an excellent gift for teaching and edifying the Body of Christ.
2. The gift of tongues is not edifying to the church unless you interpret, so the church will understand God's message.

3. However, with an interpretation, it is just as useful in bringing forth God's message.

4. Do not forbid anyone to speak in tongues.

5. In fact, He wishes we all spoke in tongues.

6. Make sure that everything is done decently and in order. God does not like confusion.

If we believe that the Scriptures are God breathed, Paul's instructions must apply to each of us.

All Scripture is God-breathed and is useful for teaching, rebuking, correcting and training in righteousness, so that the man of God may be thoroughly equipped for every good work.

2 Timothy 3:16,17 (NIV)

- **Could speaking in tongues have been isolated to the Corinthians?**

Definitely not! For one thing, God does not hide any of His gifts from the other members of the church body. He would not choose the Corinthians as a testing group. Neither would He give them any special gifts that He would not give to the rest of His Body.

More importantly, the Bible tells about other groups of believers who spoke in tongues:

A. Those who were waiting in the upper room on the day of Pentecost (Acts 2:4)

B. Those at the house of Cornelius who heard Peter speak God's Word (Acts 10:46)

C. Those at Ephesus where Paul spoke (Acts 19:6)

INTERPRETATION OF TONGUES

- **Could you give me a brief explanation of this gift?**

The interpretation of tongues is the supernatural interpretation of a message in tongues. After hearing a message spoken in tongues, a person who does not understand the tongue spoken will provide its interpretation in his own language through the power of the Holy Spirit. Then all those present can understand and be edified.

This gift acts in conjunction with the gift of divers kinds of tongues.

- **Show me some examples of this gift.**

The best example for using interpretation of tongues is included in the apostle Paul's writing to the Corinthians. They had begun having church services, and the gifts were being manifested regularly. The problem was that they had no instruction on the proper use of spiritual gifts.

The purpose of interpretation of tongues is made clear in the portion of Scripture discussed below.

The Corinthians

...**Since you are eager to have spiritual gifts, try to excel in gifts that build up the church.**

For this reason anyone who speaks in a tongue should pray that *he may interpret* what he says.

1 Corinthians 14:12,13 (NIV)

If any man speak in an unknown tongue, let it be by two, or at the most by three, and that by course; and let one *interpret*.

1 Corinthians 14:27

As we discussed earlier, this gift is very important because together with a message in tongues, it edifies the church.

- **Why is it that sometimes the message in tongues and the interpretation differ so much in length?**

Remember, the gift is called "interpretation" of tongues, not "translation." A translation is a direct, word-for-word conversion from one language to another. An interpretation may not be exactly word for word, but it gives the same message.

The interpretation will be a little different depending on the person giving it. One person, who is relatively quiet, may interpret the message in a way that is short and to the point. Another person, who tends to be more expressive, may give much more feeling with the interpretation.

This is hard for some people to grasp, so let's try a simple example. Let's say that I speak only Spanish and that I'm attempting to communicate with an individual who speaks only English. To help us communicate there are two interpreters.

I am asked this question: "How many children do you have?"

In response, I answer, "Tres" (which is Spanish for "three").

One interpreter may simply respond to my English friend by saying, "Three." The other interpreter, being a little more expressive, may say, "He has three children."

Do you see how the content of the message is exactly the same, yet the actual words are somewhat different?

This is one reason for the difference in length of the message in tongues and the interpretation.

Another possibility is incorporated into the unknown language itself. How do we know how many syllables are required to equal one word in our own language? Let's try another example.

The following questions convey the same message in two different languages, but they are different in length and syllables:

Spanish: *Como esta usted?* (3 words, 6 syllables)

English: *How are you?* (3 words, 3 syllables)

Can you see how a different language (especially when unknown) may vary considerably in length from the interpretation in your own language?

Don't try to analyze God. His ways are far above ours.

- ## Are tongues and interpretations rehearsed?

Absolutely not! These spiritual gifts are the result of individuals being led by the Holy Spirit. He provides the message that the Lord has for His Body, and an individual merely speaks it forth.

If you have ever watched people deliver a message in tongues or give the interpretation, you have never seen them holding anything like a cue card in their hands to read from. In fact, most of the time their eyes are closed. In some cases, the speaker talks for such a long time that it would be impossible for him to have memorized that message.

- ## Can an interpretation of tongues include a word of wisdom or word of knowledge?

I can find no reason that would prevent an interpretation of tongues from including a word of wisdom or a word of knowledge. Remember, God will reward His *message* for the edifying of the Church. What differs is the *method* (prophecy or tongues and interpretation).

- ## If tongues needs the gift of interpretation, should we still speak in tongues during private devotions?

First, let's clear up a misunderstanding. It is the "gift of divers tongues" used in a corporate setting (i.e. church) which needs the "gift of interpretation."

When you speak out a message in tongues for a body of believers, an interpretation is needed so that everyone in that body will be edified. Scripture confirms this:

> **If any man speak in an unknown tongue, let it be by two, or at the most by three, and that by course; and let one interpret.**
> **1 Corinthians 14:27**

Why is this necessary? Because, otherwise, speaking in tongues will edify the speaker but not the body. In order to edify that body, the interpretation of the tongues *must* be given.

> **For he that speaketh in an unknown tongue speaketh not unto men, but unto God: for no man understandeth him; howbeit in the spirit he speaketh mysteries.**
>
> **1 Corinthians 14:2**

Notice the first part of this verse says that, when we speak in tongues, we speak **not unto men, but unto God.** So the gift of interpretation is provided to interpret this message into words so that all those present can understand.

This is why the apostle Paul instructs the Corinthians to keep quiet unless they have an interpreter:

> **But if there be no interpreter, let him keep silence in the church; and let him speak to himself, and to God.**
>
> **1 Corinthians 14:28**

When you speak to yourself, you are having no effect on other people, so no interpreter would be needed. When you speak to God, He doesn't need an interpreter.

---

[1]James H. Strong, *Strong's Exhaustive Concordance*, Compact ed. (Grand Rapids: Baker, Reprinted 1992), "Hebrew and Chaldee Dictionary," p. 75, #5012.

[2]*Webster's Ninth New Collegiate Dictionary* (Springfield, MA: Merriam-Webster, 1983), p. 369.

9

Why Should You Believe Me?

In closing, let me share some thoughts.

There are two types of people who have made it to the end of this book: those who are truly seeking the Holy Spirit and eager to learn all they can about Him; and those who are doubters, looking for excuses, loopholes and "some way out."

I'm sure there is another thought on some readers' minds, the question: *Why should I believe what **he** says?*

The best way I know to answer this question is with this thought: you should not accept anything I say without question; neither should you accept what others say without question. And this includes your own church and pastor! If something sounds wrong, check it out.

What you *must* accept is what the Scriptures say — what God and Jesus say. It is up to you to read your Bible on your own and find out what They are saying.

I have included many Scriptures throughout this book to help. This is to show you that it is not me who has all the answers, but God! I am only a messenger who is attempting to help in your study. The Bible says it best:

> **Test everything. Hold on to the good.**
>
> 1 Thessalonians 5:21 (NIV)

I can only try to convince you by showing you the truth based on the Word of God. It's easy to argue with me, but not God. Even Jesus had trouble convincing some people! He said:

> **Verily, verily, I say unto thee, We speak that we do know, and testify that we have seen; and ye receive not our witness.**

If I have told you earthly things, and ye believe not, how shall ye believe, if I tell you of heavenly things?

John 3:11,12

My purpose is not to lift up *my* religion, but to lift up God, Jesus, the Holy Spirit — and *Their* promises.

I have nothing to gain by trying to deceive people, but *you* have much to gain by growing closer to God. There will be those who speak out against this book. However, it is not my purpose to please all men, but to please only God.

For the appeal we make does not spring from error or impure motives, nor are we trying to trick you. On the contrary, we speak as men approved by God to be entrusted with the gospel. We are not trying to please men but God, who tests our hearts.

1 Thessalonians 2:3,4 (NIV)

Am I now trying to win the approval of men, or of God? Or am I trying to please men? If I were still trying to please men, I would not be a servant of Christ.

I want you to know, brothers, that the gospel I preached is not something that man made up. I did not receive it from any man, nor was I taught it; rather, I received it by revelation from Jesus Christ.

Galatians 1:10-12 (NIV)

Some may have politely read this book and, just as politely, may have discarded it as an interesting "opinion" or "translation."

You may be saying to yourself about me, *That's fine for him if that's what he wants to believe.*

If that is your thought, read closely the next few paragraphs.

I have learned many things through the years. I have studied many Bible translations, read various interpretations of Scripture, heard preachers/teachers and read their books. Some I believe, some I do not.

But the baptism of the Holy Spirit is not just "something I believe." It is "something I *know*"! I know for an absolute fact that it is the Truth, that it is biblical, that it comes from Christ! That, my friend, is the bottom line.

If you are willing to take a step of faith towards Christ (not for me, but for Him), He will be faithful to fill you to overflowing with His wonderful Spirit. You too will experience the full inheritance of God! Be faithful to the Lord and follow His instructions:

> **But be ye doers of the word, and not hearers only, deceiving your own selves.**
>
> **James 1:22**

The real emphasis of the baptism of the Holy Spirit is to bring you to a new level of living for the Lord. The Holy Spirit is your Helper, Counselor and constant Companion. As you are submissive to Him, He will teach you many wonderful things. His whole purpose is to bring you closer to the Lord.

Don't quench the Spirit, but actively seek all God has for you. Ask Jesus for the baptism of the Holy Spirit. He is the Baptizer, and He will never fail.

I hope this book has been helpful in leading you to know more about the Holy Spirit, and I pray in Jesus' name that you will take it to heart.

The apostle Paul summarized it best when he asked the believers at Ephesus:

> **Have ye received the Holy Ghost since ye believed?**
>
> **Acts 19:2**

Maybe it's time...

About The Author

Steve Williamson is a minister with the Christian Evangelistic Assemblies and the founder of Mighty Wind Ministries. He holds a Bachelor of Science degree from Texas A & M University in College Station, Texas, and a Masters of Science from Southern Methodist University in Dallas.

In 1989 God placed a vision in Steve's heart to "Share the Secret of the Spirit" to the world. Mighty Wind Ministries was birthed to fulfill this vision through teaching others about the baptism in the Holy Spirit.

Steve is an anointed speaker with a heart for God and a love for people. As many will testify, he has a special gift for sharing the Holy Spirit.

Steve, his wife, Robin, and their two children are committed to sharing the love of Christ and the power of the Holy Spirit.

If you would like to contact him, please write to:

Stevan F. Williamson
Mighty Wind Ministries
P. O. Box 741906
Houston, TX 77274

*Please include your questions, prayer requests
and testimonies when you write.*

The Harrison House Vision

Proclaiming the truth and the power
Of the Gospel of Jesus Christ
With excellence;

Challenging Christians to
Live victoriously,
Grow Spiritually,
Know God intimately.